1000 Manchester United Quiz Questions

1000 Manchester United Quiz Questions

DANIEL MACDONAGH

Copyright © 2021 by Daniel MacDonagh

Print Edition

All rights reserved. No part of this publication may be reproduced, distributed or transmitted in any form or by any means, or stored in a database or retrieval system, without the prior written permission of the publisher

Table of Contents

THE EARLY YEARS 11

NAME THE THREE 13

ERIC CANTONA 14

WHERE ARE THEY FROM? 16

TRANSFERS: THE 1960S 17

NAME THE ELEVEN 18

SIR MATT BUSBY 19

APPEARANCES 21

WHO SAID THAT? 22

GEORGE BEST 25

HOW TALL? 27

FOUR OR MORE 28

SHOOT-OUTS 29

ANAGRAMS 30

BRYAN ROBSON 31

A TRICKY ONE 33

NAME THE SEASON 35

1999 CHAMPIONS LEAGUE 37

GOALSCORERS 39

WAYNE ROONEY 40

TRANSFERS: THE 1970S 42

OLD TRAFFORD 43

SIR ALEX FERGUSON 46

NAME THE SIX... 48

WHO WINS AT SCRABBLE? 49

THE DEBUT GOALSCORERS 50

NOBBY STILES 51

HOW TALL? (PART 2) 53

SHOOT-OUTS 2 54

ANAGRAMS 2 55

TRANSFERS: THE 1980S	56
NAME THE ELEVEN	57
THE GLAZERS	58
ROY KEANE	61
RECORD SIGNINGS	63
PAUL SCHOLES	64
SHOOT-OUTS 3	67
2008 CHAMPIONS LEAGUE	68
DENIS LAW	70
HAT-TRICK KINGS	72
TRANSFERS: THE 1990S	**74**
NAME THE ELEVEN	75
GARY NEVILLE	76
THE PENALTY SCORERS	78
DAVID BECKHAM	80
HOW TALL? (PART 3)	83

WHERE ARE THEY FROM? (PART 2) 84

SHOOT-OUTS 4 86

A TRICKY ONE (PART 2) 87

SIX OR MORE 90

ANAGRAMS 4 91

TRANSFERS: THE 2000S 92

NAME THE ELEVEN... 93

SIR BOBBY CHARLTON 94

CLEAN SHEETS 96

WHAT'S ERIC DONE NOW? 97

PATRICE EVRA 99

HOW TALL? (PART 4) 101

ANAGRAMS: THE MANAGERS 102

TRANSFERS: THE 2010S 103

RIO FERNINAND 104

GEORGE BEST 2 106

SHOOT-OUTS 5 108

RYAN GIGGS 109

THE CAPTAINS 111

ANSWERS 112
    Answers: The Early Years 112
    Answers: Name the Three 112
    Answers: Eric Cantona 113
    Answers: Where are they from? 113
    Answers: Transfers - The 1960s 114
    Answers: Name the Eleven 114
    Answers: Sir Matt Busby 115
    Answers: Appearances 115
    Answers: Who said that? 116
    Answers: Name the 4 116
    Answers: George Best 116
    Answers: How Tall? 117
    Answers: Four or more 118
    Answers: Shoot-outs 118
    Answers: Anagrams 118
    Answers: Bryan Robson 119
    Answers: A Tricky One 119
    Answers: Name the Season 120
    Answers: 1999 Champions League 120
    Answers: Goalscorers 121
    Answers: Wayne Rooney 121
    Answers: Transfers - The 1970s 122
    Answers: Old Trafford 123
    Answers: Sir Alex Ferguson 123
    Answers: Name the Six 124
    Answers: Who wins at Scrabble? 124
    Answers: The Debut Goalscorers 125
    Answers: Nobby Stiles 126
    Answers: How Tall? (part 2) 126
    Answers: Shoot-outs 2 127
    Answers: Anagrams 2 127
    Answers: Transfers - The 1980s 128

Answers: Name the Eleven 128
Answers: The Glazers 129
Answers: Roy Keane 129
Answers: Record Signings 130
Answers: Paul Scholes 131
Answers: Shoot-outs 3 131
Answers: 2008 Champions League 132
Answers: Denis Law 132
Answers: Hat-trick Kings 133
Answers: Anagrams 3 134
Answers: Transfers - The 1990s 134
Answers: Name the XI 135
Answers: Gary Neville 135
Answers: Penalty Scorers 136
Answers: David Beckham 137
Answers: How Tall? (part 3) 138
Answers: Where are they from? (Part 2) 138
Answers: Shoot-outs 4 139
Answers: A Tricky One (part two) 140
Answers: Name the Season 2 140
Answers: Six or more 141
Answers: Anagrams 4 142
Answers: Transfers - The 2000s 142
Answers: Name the XI 143
Answers: Sir Bobby Charlton 143
Answers: Clean Sheets 144
Answers: What's Eric done now? 145
Answers: Patrice Evra 145
Answers: How Tall? (part 4) 146
Answers: Anagrams - The Managers 146
Answers: Transfers - The 2010s 147
Answers: Rio Ferdinand 147
Answers: George Best 2 148
Answers: Shoot-outs 5 149
Answers: Ryan Giggs 149
Answers: The Captains 149

HOW DID YOU DO? 151

The Early Years

1. At which railway company's depot was the club founded?
(a) Great Northern   (b) Lancashire and Yorkshire
(c) Manchester & Sheffield

2. What was the year?
(a) 1878   (b) 1880   (c) 1882

3. Who was the club's first president?
(a) Richard Alsop   (b) Arthur Fredericks   (c) Frederick Attock

4. Where was the club's first ground?
(a) North Road   (b) West Street   (c) East Lane

5. How did the club fare in the inaugural Manchester and District Challenge Cup in 1884?
(a) knocked out in first round   (b) disqualified in the second round   (c) lost in the final

6. How many Manchester and District Challenge Cups did they win in the followimg five seasons?
(a) two   (b) three   (c) four

7. In what season did the club first enter the FA Cup?
(a) 1884-85   (b) 1886-87   (c) 1888-89

8. In what year did the club join the Football League?
(a) 1890   (b) 1892   (c) 1894

9. When did the club move to Bank Street?
(a) 1893   (b) 1895   (c) 1897

10. In what year was the club renamed Manchester United?
(a) 1900   (b) 1902   (c) 1904

11. What alternative name was considered for the club?
(a) Manchester North End   (b) Manchester Rovers
(c) Manchester Central

12. Who became club president that year?
(a) John Henry Davies   (b) David John Henry   (c) Henry Davieson

13. What was his profession?
(a) politician   (b) brewer   (c) iron works owner

14. Who was appointed manager in 1903?
(a) J.J Bentley   (b) John Chapman   (c) Ernest Mangnall

15. What was Bank Street's capacity following ground improvements in 1903-04?
(a) 30,000   (b) 40,000   (c) 50,000

16. From which scandal-hit club did United sign four players in the summer of 1906?
(a) Man City   (b) Liverpool   (c) Chelsea

17. When did United win their first league title?
(a) 1907   (b) 1908   (c) 1909

18. In what year did the club move to Old Trafford?
(a) 1908   (b) 1910   (c) 1912

19. How much did the new stadium cost?
(a) £20,000   (b) £60,000   (c) £100,000

20. In what year did United win the FA Cup for the first time?
(a) 1909 (b) 1911 (c) 1913

(Answers on page112)

Name the Three...

...Former players featured in a statue outside Old Trafford

1. _____

2. _____

3. _____

(Answers on page112)

Eric Cantona

1. In what year was Eric Cantona born?
(a) 1964   (b) 1966   (c) 1968

2. What nationality was his mother?
(a) French   (b) Italian   (c) Spanish

3. Where did he begin his faotball career, aged 14?
(a) Nimes   (b) Marseilles   (c) SO Caillolais

4. What position did he often play there?
(a) goalkeeper   (b) centre half   (c) right back

5. Why was his footballing career put on hold in 1984?
(a) he enrolled in art school   (b) to look after his grandfather   (c) so he could perform national service

6. Which was his first professional club?
(a) Nantes   (b) Auxerre   (c) Marseilles

7. Who advised him to move to England in 1991?
(a) his mother   (b) his manager   (c) his psychoanalyst

8. How long did he spend at Leeds?
(a) 10 months   (b) 12 months   (c) 14 months

9. How much did United pay for him?
(a) £900,000   (b) £1.2 million   (c) £1.5 million

10. What shirt number did he wear on his United debut on 1 December 1992?
(a) 7   (b) 8   (c) 10

11. Who were the opponents?

(a) Benfica   (b) Barcelona   (c) Bolton

12. How many goals did he score in the 1994 FA Cup final victory against Chelsea?
(a) one   (b) two   (c) three

13. Who were the opponents when Cantona was sent off at the end of a Champions League game?
(a) Juventus   (b) Fenerbahce   (c) Galatasaray

14. What shirt number did he wear for Champions League matches in the 1993-94 season?
(a) 7   (b) 9   (c) 10

15. Which Crystal Palace player did Cantona kick to earn a red card in January 1995?
(a) Marc Edworthy   (b) David Hopkin   (c) Richard Shaw

16. How long was he banned for following his assault on a Palace fan?
(a) 8 months   (b) 10 months   (c) 12 months

17. How many goals did he score for United?
(a) 82   (b) 92   (c) 102

18. How many times did he play for United?
(a) 165   (b) 185   (c) 205

19. Which side did he captain after leaving United?
(a) French 5-a-side soccer team   (b) French indoor soccer team   (c) French beach soccer team

20. Where did he become Director of Soccer in 2011?
(a) New York Cosmos   (b) LA Galaxy   (c) Leeds United

(Answers on page113)

Where are they from?
The current squad

Fill in the players' countries of birth below.

	Player	Country of Origin
1	David De Gea	
2	Alex Telles	
3	Eric Bailly	
4	Victor Lindelof	
5	Bruno Fernandes	
6	Fred	
7	Juan Mata	
8	Nemanja Matic	
9	Paul Pogba	
10	Donny van de Beek	
11	Edinson Cavani	
12	Anthony Martial	

(Answers on page 113)

Transfers: The 1960s

Match the following clubs to the United signings

Arsenal	Burnley	Chelsea	West Ham
Arsenal	Celtic	Everton	
Burnley	Chelsea	Torino	

	Date	Player	Fee	Signed from
1	Nov 1960	Noel Cantwell	£29,950	
2	Jul 1961	David Herd	£35,000	
3	Aug 1962	Denis Law	£110,000	
4	Feb 1963	Paddy Crerand	£56,000	
5	Nov 1963	Graham Moore	£35,000	
6	Apr 1964	John Connelly	£56,000	
7	May 1964	Patrick Dunne	£10,500	
8	Aug 1966	Alex Stepney	£55,000	
9	Aug 1968	Willie Morgan	£110,000	
10	Aug 1969	Ian Ure	£80,000	

(Answers on page 114)

Name the Eleven...

... United players in the 1968 European Cup final

Match the players to the shirt number they wore that day

1 _____

2 _____

3 _____

4 _____

5 _____

6 _____

7 _____

8 _____

9 _____

10 _____

11 _____

(Answers on page114)

Sir Matt Busby

1. In what year was Sir Matt born?
(a) 1904   (b) 1909   (c) 1914

2. With which club did he win his only FA Cup as a player?
(a) Preston   (b) Stoke   (c) Man City

3. Which club did Busby play for from 1936 to 1945?
(a) Newcastle   (b) Liverpool   (c) Arsenal

4. Which branch of the armed forces did he serve in during WW2?
(a) army   (b) navy   (c) air force

5. How many caps did he earn for Scotland?
(a) one   (b) five   (c) nine

6. When was he appointed United manager?
(a) Nov 1944   (b) Oct 1945   (c) Mar 1946

7. Who were the opponents when United won the FA Cup in 1948?
(a) Huddersfield   (b) West Ham   (c) Blackpool

8. Which team did he also manage in the summer of 1948?
(a) England   (b) Scotland   (c) Great Britain

9. In which season did he win his first League title?
(a) 1949-50   (b) 1951–52   (c) 1953–54

10. Which club offered him the manager's job in 1956?
(a) Real Madrid   (b) Juventus   (c) Borussia Monchengladbach

11. What honour was he awarded in 1958?
(a) OBE   (b) MBE   (c) CBE

12. In which Beatles album is Busby mentioned?
(a) Revolver   (b) Magical Mystery Tour   (c) Let It Be

13. In what year did he retire as manager?
(a) 1969   (b) 1970   (c) 1971

14. When did he received his knighthood?
(a) 1968   (b) 1978   (c) 1988

15. What position did he assume at the club in 1980?
(a) vice-chairman   (b) vice-president   (c) president

(Answers on page 115)

Appearances

Can you name the players who have made the most appearances for United?

	Player	Position	Years at club	Apps
1		Winger	1991–14	**963**
2		Forward	1956–73	**758**
3		Midfielder	1994–13	**718**
4		Centre-half	1952–70	**688**
5		Full-back	1992–11	**602**
6		Forward	2004–17	**559**
7		Goalkeeper	1966–78	**539**
8		Full-back	1960–73	**535**
9		Full-back	1990–02	**529**
10		Outside-right	1919–33	**510**

(Answers on page 115)

Who said that?

1. "Manchester is my heaven."
(a) Eric Cantona   (b) Ryan Giggs   (c) Sir Matt Busby

2. "I've never played for a draw in my life."
(a) Sir Alex Ferguson   (b) Sir Matt Busby   (c) Louis van Gaal

3. "Manchester United have always stood up again and bounced back; it's just in the DNA."
(a) David Moyes   (b) Ole Gunnar Solskjaer   (c) Sir Alex Ferguson

4. "When I think football, I think Manchester United. I still support United and always will. I will die with them in my heart."
(a) Paul Scholes   (b) Eric Cantona   (c) Lou Macani

5. "The most beautiful sight in football is to watch Manchester United chase a game."
(a) Teddy Sheringham   (b) Rio Ferdinand   (c) Jose Mourinho

6. "The work of a team should always embrace a great player but the great player must always work."
(a) Sir Matt Busby   (b) Ron Atkinson   (c) Sir Alex Ferguson

7. "I'm not at Manchester United to keep everyone happy."
(a) Eric Cantona   (b) Roy Keane   (c) David Moyes

8. "Steve Jobs was Apple; Sir Alex Ferguson is Manchester United."
(a) Avram Glazer   (b) Martin Edwards   (c) David Gill

9. "It's a special club. It's got history. When I slip on the Manchester United shirt, it's like I'm wearing its past. So you have to sacrifice yourself for this club."
(a) Patrice Evra   (b) Gary Neville   (c) Norman Whiteside

10. "You can't applaud a referee."
(a) Sir Alex Ferguson   (b) David Beckham   (c) Eric Cantona

11. "Manchester United breathe football. When I have to make hard decisions, I always listen to little boy inside me and what he wants. That little boy was screaming for United."
(a) Patrice Evra   (b) Robin van Persie   (c) Gary Pallister

12. "I thought I would be at United for a couple of years, maybe three or four, and then go abroad somewhere. But I just fell in love with Manchester United. I fell in love with winning, fell in love with the history of the club and being part of it was something I could never have imagined."
(a) Juan Mata   (b) David de Gea   (c) Rio Ferdinand

13. "I do believe in fate."
(a) Eric Cantona   (b) Sir Alex Ferguson   (c) Ole Gunnar Solskjaer

14. "I never wanted Manchester United to be second to anybody. Only the best would be good enough."
(a) Ryan Giggs   (b) Roy Keane   (c) Sir Matt Busby

15. "I know the city and the club, and I can tell you that when you play for Manchester United at Old Trafford, you no longer need to see the sunshine every day."
(a) Patrice Evra   (b) Fred   (c) Quinton Fortune

(Answers on page 116)

Name the Four...

… United players who scored own goals in the 2020-21 season

	Player	Date	Competition	Opponent	F	A
1		6 May 2021	UEFA Cup	Roma	2	3
2		26 Dec 2020	Prem Lge	Leicester	2	2
3		20 Oct 2020	Cham Lge	PSG	2	1
4		17 Oct 2020	Prem Lge	Newcastle	4	1

(Answers on page 116)

George Best

1. Where was George Best born?
(a) Ballymena   (b) Belfast   (c) Derry

2. Why was he rejected by his local club, Glentoran, as a schoolboy?
(a) for being the wrong religion   (b) for lack of ability
(c) for being too small and light

3. How old was he when he joined United?
(a) 13   (b) 15   (c) 17

4. Where did he work for two years before signing as a professional for United?
(a) Manchester Ship Canal   (b) Salford Docks
(c) the Co-op

5. In what season did he make his first-team debut?
(a) 1962-63   (b) 1963-64   (c) 1964-65

6. How tall was he?
(a) 5ft 8   (b) 5ft 9   (c) 5ft 10

7. Who were the opponents when he scored his debut goal?
(a) Burnley   (b) Stoke   (c) Liverpool

8. What number did he wear in his debut season?
(a) 7   (b) 9   (c) 11

9. Who were the opponents when a 19-year-old Best scored twice the European Cup quarter-final away leg in March 1966?
(a) Benfica   (b) Real Madrid   (c) Porto

10. What did the foreign media dub him following that performance?
(a) El Beatle   (b) the fifth Beatle   (c) El Magico

11. Which award was a 21-year-old Best the youngest ever recipient of in 1968?
(a) PFA Player of the Year   (b) BBC Goal of the Season   (c) FWA Footballer of the Year

12. How did he relax before the 1968 European Cup final?
(a) playing golf   (b) by meditating   (c) by sleeping with a woman

13. Which of United's extra-time goals did he score?
(a) first   (b) second   (c) third

14. How many goals did he score in the 8–2 win in the fifth round of the FA Cup in February 1970?
(a) five   (b) six   (c) seven

15. Who were the opponents?
(a) Northampton   (b) Wrexham   (c) Carlisle

(Answers on page 116)

How Tall?

Guess the heights of the 2020-21 squad members.

	Player	Height
1	David de Gea	
2	Victor Lindelof	
3	Eric Bailly	
4	Harry Maguire	
5	Paul Pogba	
6	Edinson Cavani	
7	Juan Mata	
8	Anthony Martial	
9	Marcus Rashford	
10	Mason Greenwood	
11	Fred	
12	Bruno Fernandes	
13	Daniel James	
14	Luke Shaw	
15	Dean Henderson	
16	Alex Telles	
17	Aaron Wan-Bissaka	
18	Nemanja Matic	
19	Donny van de Beek	
20	Scott McTominay	

Score half a point if you're an inch out either way. Half inches are rounded up.

The author accepts no responsibility for the use of platform shoes.

(Answers on page117)

Four or more

Name the United players who have scored four or more goals in a game.

	Player	Goals	Date	Opponents
1		4	26 Nov 1966	Sunderland
2		4	2 Oct 1968	Waterford
3		6	7 Feb 1970	Northampton
4		4	20 Feb 1971	Southampton
5		5	4 Mar 1995	Ipswich
6		4	6 Feb 1999	Notts Forest
7		4	3 Nov 2004	Sparta Praha
8		4	3 Dec -2008	Blackburn
9		4	23 Jan 2010	Hull City
10		5	27 Nov 2010	Blackburn

(Answers on page 118)

Shoot-outs

2005 FA Cup final
Millenium Stadium, Sat 21 May
United 0 -0 **Arsenal**

Lineup: Carroll, Brown, Ferdinand, Silvestre, O'Shea, Fletcher, Keane, Scholes, Ronaldo, van Nistelrooy, Rooney,
Subs: Fortune, Giggs,

Fill in in the names of United's penalty takers below

	United		4-5	Arsenal	
1		scored		Lauren	scored
2		saved		Ljungberg	scored
3		scored		van Persie	scored
4		scored		Cole	scored
5				Vieira	scored

Score half a point if you select a correct player but in the wrong order.

(Answers on page118)

Anagrams

Rearrange the letters to form the names of famous United players (years they were at the club in brackets).

1. Nibbles toys _ _ _ _ _ / _ _ _ _ _
   (1959–1971)

2. A swindle _ _ _ _ _ / _ _ _
   (1962–1973)

3. Begets ogre _ _ _ _ _ _ / _ _ _ _
   (1963–1974)

4. Sleepy texan _ _ _ _ / _ _ _ _ _ _ _
   (1966–1979)

5. Edgy Larry _ _ _ _ _ / _ _ _ _
   (1973–1977)

6. Anus prostrate _ _ _ _ _ _ / _ _ _ _ _ _ _
   (1974–1979)

7. Machismo tyke _ _ _ _ _ _ / _ _ _ _ _ _
   (1978–1981)

8. Sink warily _ _ _ / _ _ _ _ _ _ _
   (1979–1984)

9. Some miser _ _ _ _ / _ _ _ _ _
   (1981–1988)

10. Drongo trashcan _ _ _ _ _ _ / _ _ _ _ _ _ _ _
    (1984–1989)

(Answers on page 118)

Bryan Robson

1. In which county was Bryan Robson born?
(a) Yorkshire   (b) Northumberland   (c) Durham

2. Which club did he first play for?
(a) West Brom   (b) Newcastle   (c) Carlisle

3. What year did he sign for United?
(a) 1980   (b) 1981   (c) 1982

4. What was the fee?
(a) £1,000,000   (b) £1,250,000   (c) £1,500,000

5. Who were the opponents in 1983 League Cup semi-final in which Robson tore his ankle ligaments?
(a) Chelsea   (b) Everton   (c) Arsenal

6. How many goals did he score in the 3-0 quarter-final defeat of Barcelona in the 1983-84 Cup Winners Cup?
(a) one   (b) two   (c) three

7. How many FA Cups did he win as United captain?
(a) one   (b) two   (c) three

8. How many years was the contract he signed in 1984 for?
(a) three   (b) five   (c) seven

9. How many appearances did he make for United?
(a) 361   (b) 461   (c) 561

10. How many goals did he score at United?
(a) 77   (b) 88   (c) 99

11. At which club did he become player-manager in 1984?
(a) West Brom   (b) Bradford   (c) Middlesbrough

12. Which was the last club he managed?
(a) Leeds   (b) Sheffield United   (c) Sheffield Wednesday

13. Which national side did he take charge of in 2009?
(a) Thailand   (b) Malaysia   (c) Japan

14. What nickname did he earn at United?
(a) Superman   (b) Captain Marvel   (c) Incredible Hulk

15. What honour did he receive in 1990?
(a) MBE   (b) OBE   (c) CBE

(Answers on page 119)

A Tricky One

Match the players below to the games they scored a hat-trick.

Dimitar Berbatov	Andrei Kanchelskis	Michael Owen	Lee Sharpe
Andrew Cole	Anthony Martial	Marcus Rashford	Teddy Sheringham
Mark Hughes	Brian McClair	Cristiano Ronaldo	Carlos Tevez
Zlatan Ibrahimovic	Ruud van Nistelrooy	Wayne Rooney	Robin van Persie
Shinji Kagawa	Jesper Olsen	Paul Scholes	Dwight Yorke

	Player	Opponents	Date
1		RB Leipzig	28 Oct 2020
2		Sheffield United	24 Jun 2020
3		Saint Etienne	16 Feb 2017
4		Aston Villa	22 Apr 2013
5		Norwich	2 Mar 2013
6		Wigan	26 Dec 2011
7		Arsenal	28 Aug 2011
8		Wolfsburg	8 Dec 2009
9		Blackburn	3 Dec 2008
10		Newcastle	12 Jan 2008
11		Fulham	22 Mar 2003
12		Arsenal	25 Feb 2001
13		Southampton	28 Oct 2000
14		West Ham	1 Apr 2000
15		Feyenoord	5 Nov 1997

16		Man City	10 Nov 1994
17		Southampton	23 Jan 1991
18		Arsenal	28 Nov 1990
19		Derby	2 Apr 1988
20		West Brom	22 Feb 1986

For a 5 point bonus, can you identify the player who scored four goals in the game?

(Answers on page119)

Name the Season

1. Mikael Silvestre signs from Inter. John Curtis leaves for Blackburn. United beat West Ham 7-1 in the league.

2. Arnold Muhren signs from Ipswich on a free. United visit Wembley three times.

3. United take part in the first-ever Watney Cup before the season starts. United draw 4-4 at Derby on Boxing Day. Two Brian Kidd goals is not enough to avoid a semi-final defeat.

4. Peter Schmeichel joins from Bronby. In December Ryan Giggs scores the sixth in a 6-3 win at Oldham. United win their first-ever League Cup.

5. United are knocked out of the UEFA Cup on penalties by Videoton. Kevin Moran makes an FA Cup first.

6. United are knocked out of the Uefa Cup in the second round by Juventus. Gordon Hill scores a hat-trick in a 7-2 defeat of Newcastle in the League Cup.

7. United win the Premier League but lose in the League Cup final. The club break the English transfer record for the third time in just over a year.

8. The season starts with a new manager and a record signing. United draw 18 games in the League and finish eighth.

9. Dion Dublin signs from Cambridge. United are knocked out of the Uefa Cup on penalties and exit the FA Cup in the fifth round at Bramall Lane. David Beckham makes his debut.

10. United start the season with eight draws and a defeat. A 17-year-old from Torquay makes an impact. United lose to Forest in the FA Cup quarter-finals.

(Answers on page 120)

1999 Champions League

1. Who were United's opponents in the second qualifying round?
(a) HJK   (b) FK Obilic   (c) LKS Lodz

2. What was the score in the opening group stage game v Barcelona?
(a) 2-2   (b) 3-3   (c) 4-4

3. Who scored United's second in the 2-2 draw in Munich?
(a) Scholes   (b) Beckham   (c) Giggs

4. What was the aggregate score in United's games v Bronby?
(a) 8-1   (b) 9-3   (c) 11-2

5. Who scored the United goal in the final group match v Bayern?
(a) Sheringham   (b) Keane   (c) Scholes

6. Who scored both United goals in the quarter-final first leg v Inter?
(a) Yorke   (b) Cole   (c) Giggs

7. What was the aggregate score of the quarter-final tie?
(a) 2-1   (b) 3-1   (c) 3-2

8. How much time had been played when Giggs equalised in the semi-final first leg?
(a) 90+1   (b) 90+2   (c) 90+3

9. How much time had been played when Juventus went 2-0 up in the second leg?
(a) 7mins   (b) 9mins   (c) 11mins

10. How long did it take United to level the score?
(a) 21mins   (b) 23mins   (c) 25mins

11. What song did opera singer Montserrat Caballe perform prior to kick-off in the final?
(a) Nessun Dorma   (b) We Are The Champions   (c) Barcelona

12. What was the attendance?
(a) 90,245   (b) 94,245   (c) 98,245

13. Who picked up the only yellow card of the game?
(a) Michael Tarnat   (b) Stefan Effenberg   (c) Ronny Johnsen

14. How long had Solskjaer been on the pitch when the scored the winner?
(a) 9mins   (b) 11mins   (c) 13mins

15. Who was United's top scorer in the Champions League that season?
(a) Andy Cole   (b) Ryan Giggs   (c) Dwight Yorke

(Answers on page120)

Goalscorers

Name the players who have scored the most times for United.

	Player	Years at club	Games	Goals
1		2004–17	559	**253**
2		1956–73	758	**249**
3		1962–73	404	**237**
4		1937–55	424	**211**
5		1952–62	293	**179**
		1963–74	470	**179**
7		1919–33	510	**168**
		1991–14	963	**168**
9		1983–86 1988–95	467	**163**
10		1994–13	718	**155**

(Answers on page 121)

Wayne Rooney

1. In what year was Wayne Rooney born?
(a) 1983   (b) 1985   (c) 1987

2. How many goals did a nine-year-old Rooney score in his last season with Copplehouse Boys' Club?
(a) 77   (b) 88   (c) 99

3. How many goals did he score in his 29 games for Everton's under-10s and 11s?
(a) 84   (b) 114   (c) 144

4. How old was he when he became the Premier League's youngest ever goal scorer?
(a) 16 years, 160 days   (b) 16 years, 360 days
(c) 17 years, 60 days

5. In what year was he named BBC Young Sports Personality of the Year?
(a) 2000   (b) 2002   (c) 2004

6. When did he sign for United?
(a) Aug 2003   (b) Aug 2004   (c) Aug 2005

7. What was the transfer fee?
(a) £21.8 million   (b) £25.6 million   (c) £28.1 million

8. Who were the opponents when he scored a hat-trick on his United debut?
(a) Benfica   (b) Lyon   (c) Fenerbahce

9. What was his shirt number in his first three seasons at United?
(a) 8   (b) 9   (c) 10

10. Why was he sent off in the Champions League game against Villarreal in September 2005?
(a) for pulling a face   (b) for swearing   (c) for clapping sarcastically

11. How many goals did he score for United?
(a) 203   (b) 233   (c) 253

12. How many assists did he have for United in the Premier League?
(a) 83   (b) 103   (c) 123

13. How many goals did he score in his 120 games for England?
(a) 33   (b) 43   (c) 53

14. In what season did he win both the PFA Players' Player of the Year and the FWA Footballer of the Year awards?
(a) 2007-08   (b) 2009–10   (c) 2012-13

15. Which American club did he sign for in 2018?
(a) L.A Galaxy   (b) D.C United   (c) Salt Lake City

(Answers on page121)

Transfers: The 1970s

Match the following clubs to the United signings.

Arsenal	Celtic	Millwall	Stoke
Aberdeen	Chelsea	Notts Forest	Tottenham
Bohemians	Hull	Partick Thistle	Tranmere
Bournemouth	Leeds	Shelbourne	Wolves
Brentford	Man City	Shrewsbury	Wrexham

	Date	Player	Fee	Signed from
1	Feb 1972	Martin Buchan	£125,000	
2	Mar 1972	Ian Storey-Moore	£200,000	
3	Sep 1972	Wyn Davies	£60,000	
4	Sep 1972	Ted MacDougall	£194,000	
5	Dec 1972	Alex Forsyth	£100,000	
6	Dec 1972	George Graham	£120,000	
7	Jan 1973	Jim Holton	£84,000	
8	Jan 1973	Lou Macari	£200,000	
9	Apr 1973	Gerry Daly	£20,000	
10	Oct 1973	Paddy Roche	£15,000	
11	Dec 1973	Stewart Houston	£55,000	
12	Mar 1974	Jim McCalliog	£60,000	
13	May 1974	Stuart Pearson	£200,000	
14	Nov 1975	Gordon Hill	£70,000	
15	Dec 1975	Steve Coppell	£60,000	
16	Oct 1976	Chris McGrath	£30,000	
17	Nov 1976	Jimmy Greenhoff	£111,000	
18	Jan 1978	Joe Jordan	£350,000	
19	Nov 1978	Mickey Thomas	£333.000	
20	Aug 1979	Ray Wilkins	£778,000	

(Answers on page 122)

Old Trafford

1. Who was the United chairman when the club moved to Old Trafford?
(a) David John Henry   (b) Henry David Johns   (c) John Henry Davies

2. Which architect designed the stadium?
(a) Charles Swain   (b) Archibald Leitch   (c) J. J. Webster

3. What was the capacity when in opened?
(a) 70,000   (b) 80,000   (c) 90,000

4. When did the stadium's inaugural game take place?
(a) 8 March 1907   (b) 29 August 1908   (c) 19 February 1910

5. Who were the opponents?
(a) Liverpool.   (b) Bolton   (c) Arsenal

6. What was the capacity of the Stretford End when it was first built?
(a) 20,000   (b) 23,000   (c) 26,000

7. What is Old Trafford's record attendance?
(a) 74,962   (b) 76,962   (c) 78,962

8. In what year did the stadium host an FA Cup final (excluding replays)?
(a) 1915   (b) 1936   (c) 1952

9. In what year was the roof added to the United Road stand?
(a) 1926   (b) 1936   (c) 1946

10. What is the record post-War attendance?
(a) 74,098   (b) 75,098   (c) 76,098

11. What is the lowest post-War attendance for a competitive game?
(a) 11,968   (b) 13,968   (c) 15,968

12. What was the record aggregate attendance set in the 2008-09 season?
(a) 1,897,429   (b) 2,197,429   (c) 2,497,429

13. In what year was the first game under floodlights played?
(a) 1957   (b) 1959   (c) 1961

14. In what year was the United Road stand replaced with a cantilever stand?
(a) 1965   (b) 1966   (c) 1967

15. What "first" did the stand contain?
(a) heated seats   (b) a restaurant   (c) executive boxes

16. What was the capacity of the new North Stand when it opened in May 1996?
(a) 21,000   (b) 23,000   (c) 25,000

17. How much did it cost?
(a) £15.65m   (b) £18.65m   (c) £21.65m

18. Who were the opponents for the last game played in front of the old Stretford End in May 1992?
(a) Newcastle   (b) Aston Villa   (c) Tottenham

19. In what year was the South Stand was renamed the Sir Bobby Charlton Stand?
(a) 2012   (b) 2014   (c) 2016

20. What are the current dimensions of the Old Trafford pitch?
(a) 115 x 74 yards   (b) 112 x 76 yards   (c) 117 x 72 yards

(Answers on page123)

Sir Alex Ferguson

1. In what year was Sir Alex Ferguson born?
(a) 1939   (b) 1941   (c) 1943

2. In which district of Glasgow was he born and raised?
(a) Gorbals   (b) Partick   (c) Govan

3. What is his middle name?
(a) Norman   (b) Chapman   (c) Gordon

4. Which was the first club he played for?
(a) Queen's Park   (b) St Johnstone   (c) Dundee United

5. What did he name the Glasgow club he bought in 1978?
(a) Fergie's   (b) The Ranger   (c) The Thistle

6. Which was the first club he managed?
(a) Raith Rovers   (b) Falkirk   (c) East Stirlingshire

7. When was he sacked by St Mirren?
(a) 1974   (b) 1976   (c) 1978

8. How many league titles did he win at Aberdeen?
(a) one   (b) two   (c) three

9. When was he appointed United manager?
(a) February 1986   (b) November 1986   (c) March 1987

10. Who was his first signing as United
(a) Brian McClair   (b) Steve Bruce   (c) Viv Anderson

11. Who was his last?
(a) Wilfried Zaha   (b) Alexander Buttner   (c) Guillermo Varela

12. Why was he fined 10,000 Swiss francs by Uefa in 2003?
(a) for insulting an Uefa official   (b) for insulting a referee   (c) for claiming the Champions League draw was fixed

13. How many Premier League titles did he win?
(a) 11   (b) 12   (c) 13

14. According to analysis by the BBC, how long was "Fergie time"?
(a) 37 secs   (b) 1min 19secs   (c) 2min 5secs

15. How many times was he named Premier League manager of the season?
(a) 7   (b) 9   (c) 11

16. How many competitive matches did he manage at United?
(a) 1,300   (b) 1,400   (c) 1,500

17. At which university did he take up a long-term teaching position in April 2014?
(a) Harvard   (b) Yale   (c) Cambridge

18. What is his home in Wilmslow, Fairfields, named after?
(a) the first horse he owned   (b) a team he played for as a schoolboy   (c) the shipyard his father worked.

19. When was he awarded his knighthood?
(a) 1997   (b) 1999   (c) 2001

20. What political event is he reportedly most fascinated with?
(a) The attack on Pearl Harbor   (b) the JFK assassination
(c) the fall of the Roman Empire

(Answers on page 123)

Name the Six...

... pairs of brothers who have played for United since the war. The years they played for the club are listed below.

1. 1973-1980 & 1976-1980   _____

2. 1972-1983 & 1973   _____

3. 1992-2011 & 1995-2005   _____

4. 2005-2008 & 2008-2009   _____

5. 2008-2015 & 2008-2014   _____

6. 2011-2015 & 2011-2016   _____

(Answers on page 124)

Who wins at Scrabble?

Name the five players in the current United squad whose names would produce the highest Scrabble score.

1. _____ 33 points

2. _____ 30 points

3. _____ 28 points

4. _____ 25 points

5. _____ 25 points

And which names would produce the lowest?

1. _____ 8 points

2. _____ 13 points

3. _____ 14 points

4. _____ 16 points

5. _____ 16 points

How to score:
1 point: A E I L N O R S T U
2 points: D G
3 points: B C M P
4 points: F H V W Y.
5 points: K
8 points: J X
10 points Q Z

(Answers on page 124)

The Debut Goalscorers

Name the players who scored on their United debut.

	Player	G	Date	Comp	Opponents	F	A
1		2	6 Oct 1956	Div1	Charlton (H)	4	2
2		1	18 Aug 1962	Div1	West Brom (H)	2	2
3		1	20 Jan 1973	Div1	West Ham (H)	2	2
4		1	25 Aug 1984	Div1	Watford (H)	1	1
5		1	19 Aug 1989	Div1	Arsenal (H)	4	1
6		1	5 Jan 1993	FAC	Bury (H)	2	0
7		2	21 Sep 1994	LgeC	Port Vale (A)	2	1
8		1	25 Aug 1996	PremL	Blackburn (H)	2	2
9		1	12 Aug 2001	ChSh	Liverpool	1	2
10		1	31 Jan 2004	PremL	South'ton (H)	3	2
11		3	28 Sep 2004	ChamL	Fen'bahce (H)	6	2
12		1	7 Jan 2007	FAC	Aston Villa (H)	2	1
13		1	5 Apr 2009	PremL	Aston Villa (H)	3	2
14		1	8 Aug 2010	ChSh	Chelsea	3	1
15		2	6 May 2014	PremL	Hull City (H)	3	1
16		2	25 Feb 2016	UefaC	Midtjylland (H)	5	1
17		1	7 Aug 2016	ChSh	Leicester	2	1
18		1	8 Aug 2017	SupC	Real Madrid	1	2
19		1	11 Aug 2019	PremL	Chelsea (H)	4	0
20		1	19 Sep 2020	PremL	Crystal P (H)	1	3

(Answers on page125)

Nobby Stiles

1. In which district of Manchester was Nobby Stiles born?
(a) Longsight   (b) Davyhulme   (c) Collyhurst

2. What unexpected event was taking place during his birth?
(a) an air raid   (b) a flood   (c) a riot

3. In which season did he makes his United debut?
(a) 1958-59   (b) 1960-61   (c) 1962-63

4. How many appearances did he make for United?
(a) 295   (b) 395   (c) 495

5. How many goals did he score at United?
(a) 9   (b) 19   (c) 29

6. How many England caps did he earn?
(a) 28   (b) 38   (c) 48

7. What was he holding in his hand when he danced with World Cup trophy after the final in 1966?
(a) his medal   (b) his glasses   (c) his false teeth

8. How many appearances did he make in the 1970 World Cup?
(a) none   (b) one   (c) two

9. How many League titles did he win?
(a) one   (b) two   (c) three

10. In what year did he leave United?
(a) 1971   (b) 1972   (c) 1973

11. Which club did he join?
(a) Sunderland   (b) Newcastle   (c) Middlesbrough

12. Where did he finish his playing career?
(a) Bury   (b) Bolton   (c) Preston

13. What was the last club he managed?
(a) West Brom   (b) Stoke   (c) Notts County

14. Which Leeds footballer was Stiles' brother-in-law?
(a) Peter Lorimer   (b) Johnny Giles   (c) Billy Bremner

15. What honour was he awarded in 2000?
(a) MBE   (b) OBE   (c) CBE

(Answers on page 126)

How Tall? (part 2)

Guess the heights of these former United players.

	Player	Years at club	Height
1	Bobby Charlton	1956–1973	
2	Nobby Stiles	1959–1971	
3	Denis Law	1962–1973	
4	George Best	1963–1974	
5	Alex Stepney	1966–1979	
6	Sammy McIlroy	1971–1982	
7	Martin Buchan	1972–1983	
8	Lou Macari	1973–1984	
9	Gerry Daly	1973–1977	
10	Brian Greenhoff	1973–1979	
11	Arthur Albiston	1974–1988	
12	Steve Coppell	1975–1983	
13	Jimmy Greenhoff	1976–1980	
14	Joe Jordan	1978–1981	
15	Gordon McQueen	1978–1985	
16	Mickey Thomas	1978–1981	
17	Ray Wilkins	1979–1984	
18	Remi Moses	1981–1988	
19	Bryan Robson	1981–1994	
20	Norman Whiteside	1982–1989	

Score half a point if you're an inch out either way. Half inches are rounded up.

(Answers on page 126)

Shoot-outs 2

2008 Champions League final
Luzhniki Stadium, Wed 21 May
United   1-1   Chelsea

Lineup: van der Sar, Brown, Ferdinand, Vidic, Evra, Hargreaves, Carrick, Scholes, Ronaldo, Rooney, Tevez
Subs: Giggs, Nani, Anderson

Fill in in the names of United's penalty takers below

	United		6-5	Chelsea	
1		scored		Ballack	
2		scored		Belletti	
3		saved		Lampard	
4		scored		Cole	
5		scored		Terry	missed
6		scored		Kalou	
7		scored		Anelka	saved

Score half a point if you select a correct player but in the wrong order.

(Answers on page 127)

Anagrams 2

Rearrange the letters to form the names of United player. The years they were at the club are in brackets.

1. Cheer militant   _ _ _ _ _ _ _ / _ _ _ _ _ _
   (1946–1952)

2. Bullies folk   _ _ _ _ / _ _ _ _ _ _ _
   (1952–1970)

3. Dived hard   _ _ _ _ _ / _ _ _ _
   (1961–1968)

4. Wins deal   _ _ _ _ _ _ / _ _ _ _ _ _ _ _
   (1962–1973)

5. Edgy Larry   _ _ _ _ _ / _ _ _ _
   (1973–1977)

6. Minor knave   _ _ _ _ _ / _ _ _ _ _
   (1979–1988)

7. Faster plankton   _ _ _ _ _ / _ _ _ _ _ _ _ _ _
   (1981–1987)

8. Daintier showmen   _ _ _ _ _ _ / _ _ _ _ _ _ _ _ _
   (1982–1989)

9. Criminal crab   _ _ _ _ _ / _ _ _ _ _ _ _
   (1987–1998)

10. Real sheep   _ _ _ / _ _ _ _ _ _
    (1988–1996)

(Answers on page 127)

Transfers: The 1980s

Match the following clubs to the United signings.

Aberdeen	Barcelona	Everton	Torquay
Ajax	Celtic	Middlesbrough	Tottenham
Arsenal	Coventry	Norwich	Vancouver
Arsenal	Coventry	Notts Forest	West Brom
Aston Villa	Dundee United	Southampton	West Ham

	Date	Player	Fee	Signed from
1	Oct 1980	Garry Birtles	£1.25m	
2	Aug 1981	John Gidman	£450,000	
3	Aug 1981	Frank Stapleton	£900,000	
4	Sep 1981	Remi Mose	£650,000	
5	Sep 1982	Peter Beardsley	£250,000	
6	Jun 1984	Alan Brazil	£625,000	
7	Jun 1984	Jesper Olsen	£350,000	
8	Jul 1984	Gordon Strachan	£600,000	
9	Jul 1985	Peter Barnes	£50,000	
10	Nov 1985	Colin Gibson	£275,000	
11	Jan 1986	Terry Gibson	£600,000	
12	Jul 1987	Viv Anderson	£250,000	
13	Jul 1987	Brian McClair	£850,000	
14	Dec 1987	Steve Bruce	£825,000	
15	Jun 1988	Lee Sharpe	£185,000	
16	Jun 1988	Mark Hughes	£1.8m	
17	Nov 1988	Ralph Milne	£175,000	
18	Aug 1989	Gary Pallister	£2.3m	
19	Sep 1989	Paul Ince	£1.0m	
20	Sep 1989	Danny Wallace	£1.3m	

(Answers on page 128)

Name the Eleven...

... United players who started the 1991 Cup Winners' Cup final.

Match the players to the shirt number they wore that day

1 _____

2 _____

3 _____

4 _____

5 _____

6 _____

7 _____

8 _____

9 _____

10 _____

11 _____

(Answers on page 128)

The Glazers

1. Where are the Glazer family from?
(a) New York   (b) Miami   (c) Los Angeles

2. How did Malcolm Glazer start out in business?
(a) selling real estate   (b) selling insurance   (c) selling watches

3. Which NFL club do the Glazers own?
(a) Miami Dolphins   (b) Tampa Bay Buccaneers   (c) Kansas City Chiefs

4. How much did the Glazer family pay for their initial 2.9% stake purchased in March 2003?
(a) £6 million   (b) £9 million   (c) £12 million

5. What were the names of the shareholders who sold a 28.7% stake to the Glazers in May 2005?
(a) MacDonald and Magee   (b) McNeill and Molloy   (c) McManus and Magnier

6. When did Avram, Joel and Bryan Glazer become United directors?
(a) March 2004   (b) June 2005   (c) August 2006

7. How much money did they borrow to buy the club?
(a) £440 million   (b) £550 million   (c) £660 million

8. What were the annual interst payments on the debt?
(a) £22 million   (b) £42 million   (c) £62 million

9. How much of that debt was secured against the club's assets?
(a) £165-£175 million (b) £265-£275 million (c) £365-£375 million

10. When had the club last been in debt?
(a) 1917   (b) 1931   (c) 1945

11. What had the debt grown to by January 2010?
(a) £516.5 million   (b) £616.5 million   (c) £716.5 million

12. What name had been given to the group of investors who were planning a takeover in March 2010?
(a) Red Knights   (b) Shareholders United   (c) The Green & Golds

13. What was the membership of the Manchester United Supporters' Trust at that time?
(a) 85,000   (b) 125,000   (c) 165,000

14. How much did the Glazers make by floating 10% of the club's shares on the New York Stock Exchange in 2012?
(a) £35 million   (b) £55 million   (c) £75 million

15. How nuch did they make by selling 12 milllion United shares in 2015?
 (a) £69 million   (b) £99 million   (c) £129 million

16. How much did they make by selling a further 4.3million United shares in 2017?
(a) £36 million   (b) £56 million   (c) £76 million

17. What is the average annual dividend paid to the Glazers by United since 2016?
(a) £42 million   (b) £32 million   (c) £22 million

18. How much has been spent on interest and debt repayments since the Glazer takeover?
(a) £548 million   (b) £748 million   (c) £948 million

19. How much is United co-chairman Avram Glazer set to make after announcing in March 2021 that he has put some shares up for sale?
(a) £70 million   (b) £50 million   (c) £30 million

20. As of May 2021, how much are United in debt?
(a) £255.5 million   (b) £355.5 million   (c) £455.5 million

(Answers on page 129)

Roy Keane

1. Where was Roy Keane born?
(a) Dublin   (b) Cork   (c) Galway

2. At which club did he start his professional career?
(a) Cork City   (b) Galway United   (c) Cobh Ramblers

3. How much did Nottingham Forest pay to sign an 18-year-old Keane?
(a) £47,000   (b) £87,000   (c) £127,000

4. In what year did he sign for United?
(a) 1992   (b) 1993   (c) 1994

5. What was the fee?
(a) £3,750,000   (b) £4,500,000   (c) £5,250,000

6. Who were the opponents in the 1994-95 FA Cup semi-final in which Keane received his first red card as a United player?
(a) Southampton   (b) Crystal Palace   (c) Portsmouth

7. How many appearances did he make for United?
(a) 480   (b) 560   (c) 640

8. How many red cards did he receive at United?
(a) 9   (b) 11   (c) 13

9. In what year was he made United's club captain?
(a) 1995   (b) 1997   (c) 1999

10. How many goals did he score for United?
(a) 51   (b) 61   (c) 71

11. Which of the goals did he score in the 3-2 defeat of Juventus in the 1998-99 Champions League semi-final?
(a) first (b) second (c) third

12. When was he voted PFA Players' Player of the Year and FWA Footballer of the Year?
(a) 1996 (b) 1998 (c) 2000

13. Which club did he join in December 2005?
(a) Ipswich (b) Celtic (c) Hibernian

14. Which club did he become manager of in August 2006?
(a) Newcastle (b) Middlesbrough (c) Sunderland

15. What was the name of his labrador retriever, who died in 2012?
(a) Triggs (b) Woofie (c) Fergie

(Answers on page 129)

Record Signings

Nname the United signings who broke the club's transfer record.

	Player	Date	Signed from	Fee
1		Feb 1972	Aberdeen	£125,000
2		Mar 1972	Notts Forest	£200,000
3		Jan 1978	Leeds	£350,000
4		Feb 1978	Leeds	£495,000
5		Aug 1979	Chelsea	£825,000
6		Oct 1980	Notts Forest	£1,250,000
7		Oct 1981	West Brom	£1,500,000
8		Jun 1988	Barcelona	£1,800,000
9		Aug 1989	Middlesbrough	£2,300,000
10		Jul 1993	Notts Forest	£3,750,000
11		Jan 1995	Newcastle	£7,000,000
12		Jul 1998	PSV Eindhoven	£10,750,000
13		Aug 1998	Aston Villa	£12,600,000
14		Jun 2001	PSV Eindhoven	£19,000,000
15		Jul 2001	Lazio	£28,100,000
16		Jul 2002	Leeds	£29,300,000
17		Sep 2008	Tottenham	£30,750,000
18		Jan 2014	Chelsea	£37,100,000
19		Aug 2014	Real Madrid	£59,700,000
20		Aug 2016	Juventus	£89,300,000

(Answers on page 130)

Paul Scholes

1. Where was Paul Scholes born?
(a) Salford   (b) Stoke   (c) Stockport

2. In what year did he play in the FA Youth Cup final?
(a) 1991   (b) 1992   (c) 1993

3. What was his first shirt number after turning professional?
(a) 16   (b) 20   (c) 24

4. What was notable about his first-team debut, a 2-1 League Cup win v Port Vale in September 1994?
(a) he scored both goals   (b) he scored an own goal   (c) he got sent off

5. In which season did he score his first hat-trick?
(a) 1997-98   (b) 1999-2000   (c) 2002-03

6. Who were the opponents when he scored with a volley from a Beckham corner?
(a) Soithampton   (b) Bradford   (c) Middlesbrough

7. What medical issue caused him to miss the second half of the 2005–06 season?
(a) asthma   (b) foot injury   (c) blurred vision

8. For what offence did he received a second tellow card in the 2008 UEFA Super Cup against Zenit Saint Petersburg?
(a) dangerous play   (b) deliberate handball   (c) dissent

9. Who were the opponents for his testimonial in August 2011?
(a) Celtic   (b) Millonarios   (c) New York Cosmos

10. Who were the opponents for his first game back from retirement?
(a) Man City   (b) Arsenal   (c) Aston Villa

11. What was his shirt number that season?
(a) 16   (b) 22   (c) 28

12. How many appearances did he make for United?
(a) 519   (b) 619   (c) 719

13. How many yellow cards did he receive in the Premier League?
(a) 87   (b) 97   (c) 107

14. How many United goals did he score?
(a) 115   (b) 135   (c) 155

15. What are the most goals he's scored in a season in all competitions?
(a) 17   (b) 20   (c) 23

16. How many Premier League titles did he win?
(a) 9   (b) 10   (c) 11

17. How many England caps did he get?
(a) 66   (b) 76   (c) 86

18. Who were the opponents in June 1999 when Scholes became the first, and last, England player to be sent off at the old Wembley Stadium?
(a) Sweden   (b) France   (c) Spain

19. When did he join United's coaching staff?
(a) June 2013   (b) April 2014   (c) May 2015

20. For which newspaper did he become a columnist?
(a) Daily Mirror   (b) Daily Mail   (c) The Independent

(Answers on page 131)

Shoot-outs 3

2009 League Cup final
Wembley, Sun 1 Mar
United 0 -0 **Tottenham**

Lineup: Foster, O'Shea, Ferdinand, Evans, Evra, Ronaldo, Gibson, Scholes, Nani, Tevez, Welbeck
Subs: Anderson, Vidic, Giggs

Fill in in the names of United's penalty takers below.

	United		4-1	Tottenham	
1		scored		O'Hara	saved
2		scored		Corluka	scored
3		scored		Bentley	missed
4		scored			

Score half a point if you select a correct player but in the wrong order.

(Answers on page131)

2008 Champions League

1. Who were United's Portuguese opponents in the first group game?
(a) Benfica   (b) Sporting CP   (c) Porto

2. Who scored the only goal in the 1-0 win v Roma in the second group game?
(a) Rooney   (b) Scholes   (c) Ronaldo

3. What was the aggregate score in the two group games v Dynamo Kyiv?
(a) 6-0   (b) 7-1   (c) 8-2

4. How many points did United finish the group on?
(a) 14   (b) 15   (c) 16

5. Which French club did United beat in the Round of 16?
(a) Lyon   (b) Lens   (c) Lille

6. What was the aggregate score?
(a) 1-0   (b) 2-1   (c) 3-2

7. How did Ronaldo score the opening goal in the 2-0 away win v Roma in the quarter-final first leg?
(a) from a free-kick   (b) from a penalty   (c) from a header

8. Who scored the only goal of the return leg?
(a) Rooney   (b) Nani   (c) Tevez

9. How many minutes had been played when were United were awarded a penalty in the semi-final first leg?
(a) one (b) two (c) three

10. Who scored the only goal of the second leg?
(a) Hargreaves (b) Scholes (c) Carrick

11. Where was the final held?
(a) Krestovsky Stadium (b) Otkrytie Arena (c) Luzhniki Stadium

12. Who did Scholes had a mid-air collision with that left the United player with a bloodied nose?
(a) Makelele (b) Terry (c) Ballack

13. Which United player did Drogba slap in extra-time to earn his red card?
(a) Vidic (b) Evra (c) Brown

14. Who was the only United player to miss a penalty in the shoot-out?
(a) Carrick (b) Ronaldo (c) Anderson

15. Who missed Chelsea's final penalty in the shoot-out?
(a) Drogba (b) Kalou (c) Anelka

(Answers on page 132)

Denis Law

1. Where was Denis Law born?
(a) Aberdeen   (b) Glasgow   (c) Edinburgh

2. Who were the first club he played for?
(a) Hibernian   (b) Huddersfield   (c) Hull

3. What was the fee when he signed for Man City in 1960?
(a) £35,000   (b) £55,000   (c) £75,000

4. Which Italian club did he leave City for in 1961?
(a) Inter Milan   (b) Napoli   (c) Torino

5. What was the cause of non-footballing injuries he suffered in Italy in February 1962?
(a) a car crash   (b) he was hit by a scooter   (c) he fell from a balcony

6. How much did United pay to sign him in July 1962?
(a) £55,000   (b) £85,000   (c) £115,000

7. How many games did he play for United?
(a) 303   (b) 404   (c) 505

8. How many goals did he score at United?
(a) 197   (b) 217   (c) 237

9. What part of his body gave him trouble throughout his career?
(a) his knee (b) his ankle (c) his shoulder

10. In what year did he win the Ballon d'Or?
(a) 1964   (b) 1968   (c) 1972

11. How many times did he score in his 55 appearances for Scotland?
(a) 20   (b) 25   (c) 30

12. Which international footballer was named after Law?
(a) Denis Irwin   (b) Dennis Wise   (c) Dennis Bergkamp

13. How many FA Cups has he won?
(a) one   (b) two   (c) three

14. Where was a statue of Law unveiled in 2012?
(a) University of Manchester   (b) University of Aberdeen   (c) Old Trafford

15. What honour did he receive in 2016?
(a) MBE   (b) OBE   (c) CBE

(Answers on page 132)

Hat-trick Kings

Name the post-war United plays who have scored the most hat-tricks.

	Player	Born	Years at club	Total Apps	Total Goals	H-Ts
1		Scotland	1962-73	404	237	18
2		England	1937-55	424	211	12
3		England	1952-62	293	179	9
4		England	2004-17	559	253	8
5		England	1956-73	758	249	7
6		Holland	2001-06	219	150	6
7		Scotland	1961-68	265	145	6
8		England	1952-58	191	131	5
9		England	1994-02	275	121	5
10		Scotland	1956-62	93	54	4
11		Bulgaria	2008-12	149	56	4
12		Wales	1983-86 & 1988-95	467	163	4
13		N. Ireland	1963-74	470	179	4
14		Holland	2012-2015	105	58	3
15		Trinidad & Tobago	1998-2002	152	66	3
16		Norway	1996-2007	366	126	3
17		England	1977-1980	42	13	2
18		England	1958-1964	184	56	2
19		Scotland	1987-98	471	127	2
20		England	1994-13	718	155	2

(Answers on page133)

Anagrams 3

Rearrange the letters to form the names of United player. The years they were at the club are in brackets.

1. Playgirl tears   ____ / _____
   (1989–1998)

2. Vera yelling   ____ / _____
   (1992–2011)

3. Cocaine rant   ____ / _____
   (1992–1997)

4. Dehydrating hems   _____ / _____
   (1997–2001)

5. Owns brew   ___ / _____
   (1998–2001)

6. Jam tapas   ____ / ____
   (1998–2001)

7. Sleek relativism   _____ / _____
   (1999–2008)

8. Devolutionary runs ____ / ___ / _____
   (2001-2006)

9. Finer android   ___ / _____
   (2002–2014)

10. Nonracial Doritos _____ / _____
    (2003–2009)

(Answers on page 134)

Transfers: The 1990s

Match the clubs to the United signings.

Aston Villa	Blackburn	Molde	PSV Eindhoven
Atletico Madrid	Brondby	Newcastle	Shakhtar Donetsk
Barcelona	Cambridge	Notts Forest	Slavia Prague
Besiktas	Inter Milan	Oldham	Tottenham
Blackburn	Leeds	QPR	York City

	Date	Player	Fee	Signed from
1	Jun 1990	Denis Irwin	£250,000	
2	Mar 1991	Andrei Kanchelskis	£650,000	
3	Aug 1991	Peter Schmeichel	£500,000	
4	Aug 1991	Paul Parker	£2.0m	
5	Aug 1992	Dion Dublin	£1.0m	
6	Nov 1992	Eric Cantona	£1.2m	
7	Jul 1993	Roy Keane	£3.75m	
8	Jul 1994	David May	£1.4m	
9	Jan 1995	Andy Cole	£6.0m	
10	Jul 1996	Ronny Johnsen	£1.2m	
11	Jul 1996	Ole Gunnar Solskjaer	£1.5m	
12	Jul 1996	Karel Poborsky	£3.5m	
13	Aug 1996	Jordi Cruyff	£1.5m	
14	Jun 1997	Teddy Sheringham	£3.5m	
15	Aug 1997	Henning Berg	£5m	
16	Mar 1998	Jonathan Greening	£750,000	
17	Nov 1998	Jaap Stam	£10.75m	
18	Aug 1998	Dwight Yorke	£12.6m	
19	Aug 1999	Quentin Fortune	£1.5m	
20	Sep 1999	Mickael Silvestre	£4.0m	

(Answers on page 134)

Name the Eleven...

... **United players who started the 1999 Champions League final.**

Match the players to the shirt number they wore that day

1 _____

2 _____

5 _____

6 _____

3 _____

11 _____

7 _____

8 _____

15 _____

19 _____

9 _____

(Answers on page135)

Gary Neville

1. In what year was Gary Neville born?
(a) 1973   (b) 1975   (c) 1977

2. Which sport did he play for his county for as a schoolboy?
(a) cricket   (b) rugby league   (c) hockey

3. When did he make his full United debut?
(a) April 1991   (b) September 1992   (c) November 1993

4. In what year did he become club captain?
(a) 2001   (b) 2003   (c) 2005

5. How many appearances did he make for United?
(a) 502   (b) 602   (c) 702

6. Against which club did he pick up an injury in March 2007 that sidelined him for more than a year?
(a) West Ham   (b) Bolton   (c) Aston Villa

7. How many United goals did he score?
(a) 7   (b) 14   (c) 21

8. How many England caps did he earn?
(a) 65   (b) 75   (c) 85

9. How many Premier League titles did he win?
(a) 7   (b) 8   (c) 9

10. In whay year was he appointed England assistant manager?
(a) 2010   (b) 2012   (c) 2014

11. Which Grade II-listed Manchester building did he and Ryan Giggs buy for £1.5 million in 2013?
(a) Northern Stock Exchange   (b) Midland Hotel
(c) Watts Warehouse

12. Which club did he become a co-owner of in 2014?
(a) Bury   (b) FC United   (c) Salford City

13. Who awarded him an honorary doctorate of science in 2014?
(a) University of Salford   (b) University of Manchester
(c) University of Liverpool

14. Which Spanish club did he manage from December 2015 to March 2016?
(a) Athletic Bilbao   (b) Valencia   (c) Real Sociedad

15. What was the title of his 2012 autobiography?
(a) Glory, Glory   (b) Red   (c) Made in Manchester

(Answers on page 135)

The Penalty Scorers

Name the players who have scored the most penalties for United.

	Player	Born	Years at club	Apps	Pens scored
1		Holland	2001-06	219	28
2		England	2004-17	559	27
3		Portugal	2020-	74	20
4		England	1958-64	184	18
5		France	1992-97	185	18
6		England	1987-96	414	17
7		England	1946-50	162	16
8		Eire	1973-77	142	16
9		Portugal	2003-09	292	16
10		Scotland	1962-73	404	15
11		England	1951-58	280	13
12		Eire	1990-02	529	12
13		N. Ireland	1963-74	470	11
14		Scotland	1984-89	201	10
15		England	1956-73	758	9
16		England	1975-78	134	9
17		France	2011--	201	9
18		England	2016-	265	9
19		Scotland	1968-75	296	8
20		Scotland	1987-98	471	7
21		Holland	2012-15	105	7
22		France	2015-	258	7
23		Scotland	1905-11	122	6
24		England	1906-19	319	6

25		England	1928-37	180	**6**
26		N. Ireland	1971-82	419	**6**
27		Holland	1982-85	98	**6**
28		Denmark	1984-89	176	**6**
29		England	1985-89	106	**6**
30		Spain	2014-	269	**6**

(Answers on page 136)

David Beckham

1. In which London district was David Beckham born?
(a) Barnet   (b) Leytonstone   (c) Tooting

2. What role did an 11-year-old Beckham play in a United v West Ham match in 1986?
(a) ballboy   (b) West Ham mascot   (c) United mascot

3. On which birthday did he sign schoolboy forms at United?
(a) 12th   (b) 14th   (c) 16th

4. Who did United beat to win the FA Youth Cup in 1992?
(a) Crystal Palace   (b) Charlton   (c) Chelsea

5. Who did he replace as a substitute to make his first-team debut in Sept 1992?
(a) Paul Ince   (b) Lee Sharpe   (c) Andrei Kanchelskis

6. Where did he go on loan in the 1994-95 season?
(a) Bury   (b) Preston   (c) Oldham

7. What was his most memorable moment there?
(a) scoring from a corner   (b) scoring from a 35-yard free-kick   (c) getting three assists in a game

8. Who were the opponents for his Premier League debut in April 1995?
(a) Everton   (b) Arsenal   (c) Leeds

9. What was the score?
(a) 0-0   (b) 1-1   (c) 2-2

10. What shirt number was he given at the beginning of the 1996–97 season?
(a) 7   (b) 9   (c) 10

11. Who was the goalkeeper he beat from 57 yards on the opening day of the 1996-97 season?
(a) Hans Segers   (b) Neil Sullivan   (c) Dave Beasant

12. How many assists did he have in the 1997–98 Premier League season?
(a) 11   (b) 13   (c) 15

13. In what year did he marry Victoria Adams, a.k.a "Posh Spice"?
(a) 1998   (b) 1999   (c) 2000

14. How many staff were reportedly employed for the wedding?
(a) 237   (b) 337   (c) 437

15. Who were the opponents when he broke a metatarsal bone in April 2002?
(a) Bayer Leverkusen   (b) Deportivo de La Coruna   (c) Lille

16. How many England caps did he earn?
(a) 95   (b) 105   (c) 115

17. How many League titles did he win at United?
(a) five   (b) six   (c) seven

18. How many goals did he score for United from free-kicks?
(a) 20   (b) 27   (c) 34

19. Where did he finish his playing career in 2013?
(a) LA Galaxy   (b) Milan   (c) PSG

20. What honour was he awarded in 2003?
(a) MBE   (b) OBE   (c) CBE

(Answers on page137)

How Tall? (part 3)

Guess the heights of these former United players.

	Player	Years at club	Height
1	Jesper Olsen	1984–1988	
2	Gordon Strachan	1984–1989	
3	Brian McClair	1987–1998	
4	Steve Bruce	1987–1996	
5	Mal Donaghy	1988–1992	
6	Gary Pallister	1989–1998	
7	Paul Ince	1989–1995	
8	Denis Irwin	1990–2002	
9	Ryan Giggs	1991–2014	
10	Andrei Kanchelskis	1991–1995	
11	Paul Parker	1991–1996	
12	Peter Schmeichel	1991–1999	
13	Gary Neville	1992–2011	
14	David Beckham	1992–2003	
15	Nicky Butt	1992–2004	
16	Eric Cantona	1992–1997	
17	Roy Keane	1993–2005	
18	Paul Scholes	1994–2013	
19	Andy Cole	1995–2001	
20	Phil Neville	1995–2005	

Score half a point if you're an inch out either way. Half inches are rounded up.

(Answers on page 138)

Where are they from? (part 2)

In which countries were these players born?

	Player	Years at club	Ga	Gls	Country of Origin
1	Jesper Olsen	1984–1988	176	24	
2	Andrei Kanchelskis	1991–1995	161	36	
3	Peter Schmeichel	1991–1999	398	1	
4	Eric Cantona	1992–1997	185	82	
5	Ronny Johnsen	1996–2002	150	9	
6	Ole Gunnar Solskjaer	1996–2007	366	126	
7	Henning Berg	1997–2000	103	3	
8	Jaap Stam	1998–2001	127	1	
9	Dwight Yorke	1998–2002	152	66	
10	Quinton Fortune	1999–2006	126	11	
11	Mikael Silvestre	1999–2008	361	10	
12	Fabien Barthez	2000–2004	139	0	
13	Ruud van Nistelrooy	2001–2006	219	150	
14	Cristiano Ronaldo	2003–2009	292	118	
15	Louis Saha	2004–2008	124	42	
16	Edwin van der Sar	2005–2011	266	0	
17	Park Ji-sung	2005–2012	205	27	
18	Patrice Evra	2006–2014	379	10	
19	Nemanja Vidic	2006–2014	300	21	
20	Nani	2007–2015	230	40	
21	Anderson	2007–2015	181	9	
22	Dimitar Berbatov	2008–2012	149	56	
23	Rafael	2008–2015	170	5	
24	Antonio Valencia	2009–2019	339	25	
25	Javier Hernandez	2010–2015	157	59	
26	Robin van Persie	2012–2015	105	58	
27	Marouane Fellaini	2013–2019	177	22	

28	Daley Blind	2014–2018	141	6	
29	Ander Herrera	2014–2019	189	20	
30	Marcos Rojo	2014–2019	122	2	

(Answers on page138)

Shoot-outs 4

2009 FA Cup semi-final
Wembley, Sun 19 April
United   0 - 0   Everton

Lineup: Foster, Rafael da Silva, Ferdinand, Vidic, Fabio da Silva, Park, Ji-Sung, Anderson, Gibson, Welbeck, Tevez, Macheda
Subs: Evra, Scholes, Berbatov

Fill in in the names of United's penalty takers below

	United		2-4	Everton	
1		saved		Cahill	Missed
2		saved		Baines	Scored
3		scored		Neville	Scored
4		scored		Vaughn	Scored
5				Jagielka	scored

Score half a point if you select a correct player but in the wrong order.

(Answers on page 139)

A Tricky One (part 2)

Match the players to the games they scored a hat-trick in.

John Connelly	Alan Gowling	Norbert Lawton	Albert Quixall
George Best	Jimmy Greenhoff	Lou Macari	Andy Ritchie
Bobby Charlton	David Herd	Sammy McIlroy	Frank Stapleton
Gerry Daly	Gordon Hill	Willie Morgan	Dennis Viollet
Alex Dawson	Denis Law	Stuart Pearson	Norman Whiteside

	Player	Opponents	Date
1		West Ham	9 Mar 1985
2		Watford	19 Nov 1983
3		Wolves	3 Oct 1981
4		Tottenham	12 Apr 1980
5		Birmingham	20 Aug 1977
6		Newcastle	19 Feb 1977
7		Newcastle	27 Oct 1976
8		Oxford	2 Nov 1974
9		Millwall	24 Aug 1974
10		West Ham	18 Sep 1971
11		Southampton	20 Feb 1971
12		QPR	19 Mar 1969
13		Sunderland	18 Jan 1969
14		Northampton	5 Feb 1966
15		West Brom	17 Dec 1966
16		Hjk Helsinki	6 Oct 1965
17		Ipswich	7 Apr 1962
18		Notts Forest	26 Dec 1961
19		Burnley	12 Apr 1961
20		Man City	31 Dec 1960

(Answers on page140)

Name the Season 2

1. David May joins from Blackburn. There's trouble at the Palace in January and drama on the last day of the season.

2. United win their first ten league games of the season but end it in fourth. United are one of six entrants in the Football League Super Cup

3. United take on Bayern, Milan and Celtic in New York pre-season. Roy Keane and Patrick Vieira have to be pulled apart in the tunnel before a game at Highbury.

4. Steve Bruce signs for £900,000 from Norwich. United come back from 3-1 down to draw 3-3 at Anfield

5. Bryan Robson leaves the club. Eric Cantona finishes top scorer with 25 goals. Ryan Giggs is voted PFA Player of the Year.

6. United enter the Anglo-Italian Cup for the only time. Ted MacDougall signs from. Third Division Bournemouth for £194,000. December sees a a major change at the club

7. Michael Carrick signs from Tottenham. Ruud van Nistelrooy leaves for Madrid. United lose to Chelsea in the League Cup final.

8. Denis Irwin joins in the summer. United lose a League Cup final..Brian Kidd takes over from Archie Knox as assistant manager.

9. United and West Ham fans clash on a Sealink ferry in August. A fourth round defeat in the League Cup leads to a change of manager.

10. Tony Coton joins the club in January but never plays a first team game. Cantona scores a winning cup-final goal.

(Answers on page 140)

Six or more

Match the opponents below to the last 20 games where United score six or more goals.

Arsenal	Brondby	Newcastle	Southampton
Arsenal	Fenerbahce	Notts Forest	Southampton
Barnsley	Leeds	Roma	Tranmere
Blackburn	Leicester	Roma	West Ham
Bradford	Newcastle	Sheffield Wed	West Ham

	Date	Competition		Score	Opponents
1	25 Oct 1997	Prem League	H	7 - 0	
2	1 Nov 1997	Prem League	H	6 - 1	
3	21 Oct 1998	Cham League	A	6 - 2	
4	16 Jan 1999	Prem League	A	6 - 2	
5	6 Feb 1999	Prem League	A	8 - 1	
6	1 Apr 2000	Prem League	H	7 - 1	
7	5 Sep 2000	Prem League	H	6 - 0	
8	25 Feb 2001	Prem League	H	6 - 1	
9	22 Dec 2001	Prem League	H	6 - 1	
10	26 Jan 2003	FA Cup	H	6 - 0	
11	12 Apr 2003	Prem League	A	6 - 2	
12	28 Sep 2004	Cham League	H	6 - 2	
13	10 Apr 2007	Cham League	H	7 - 1	
14	12 Jan 2008	Prem League	H	6 - 0	
15	27 Nov 2010	Prem League	H	7 - 1	
16	28 Aug 2011	Prem League	H	8 - 2	
17	26 Jan 2020	FA Cup	A	6 - 0	
18	20 Dec 2020	Prem League	H	6 - 2	
19	2 Feb 2021	Prem League	H	9 - 0	
20	29 Apr 2021	UEFA Cup	H	6 - 2	

(Answers on page 141)

Anagrams 4

Rearrange the letters to form the names of United players. The years they were at the club are in brackets.

1. Oasis haul _ _ _ _ _ / _ _ _ _
   (2004–2008)

2. Invaded warrens _ _ _ _ _ / _ _ _ / _ _ _ / _ _ _
   (2005–2011)

3. Prevaricate _ _ _ _ _ _ _ / _ _ _ _
   (2006–2014)

4. NSA drone _ _ _ _ _ _ _ _
   (2007–2015)

5. Chills margins _ _ _ _ _ / _ _ _ _ _ _ _ _
   (2010–2019)

6. John's pile _ _ _ _ / _ _ _ _ _
   (2011–)

7. Proven Siberian _ _ _ _ _ / _ _ _ / _ _ _ _ _ _
   (2012–2015)

8. Libel dandy _ _ _ _ _ / _ _ _ _ _
   (2014-2018)

9. Icy liberal _ _ _ _ / _ _ _ _ _ _
   (2016–)

10. Mongoose warned _ _ _ _ _ / _ _ _ _ _ _ _ _ _
    (2019–)

(Answers on page 142)

Transfers: The 2000s

Match the clubs to the United signings.

Atletico Independiente	Monaco	PSG	Stoke
Bayern Munich	Monaco	PSV Eindhoven	Sunderland
Fulham	Nantes	PSV Eindhoven	Tottenham
Lazio	Newcastle	Spartak Moscow	Wigan
Leeds	Porto	Sporting Lisbon	Wigan

	Date	Player	Fee	Signed from
1	May 2000	Fabien Barthez	£7.8m	
2	Jul 2001	Ruud Van Nistelrooy	£19.0m	
3	Jul 2001	Juan Sebastian Veron	£28.1m	
4	Jul 2001	Roy Carroll	£2.5m	
5	Jan 2002	Diego Forlan	£7.5m	
6	Jul 2002	Rio Ferdinand	£30.0m	
7	Jul 2003	David Bellion	£2.0m	
8	Jul 2003	Eric Djemba-Djemba	£3.5m	
9	Aug 2003	Cristiano Ronaldo	£12.2m	
10	Jan 2004	Louis Saha	£12.8m	
11	Jun 2004	Gabriel Heinze	£6.9m	
12	Jul 2005	Ji-Sung Park	£4.0m	
13	Jul 2005	Ben Foster	£1.0m	
14	Jan 2006	Nemanja Vidic	£7.2m	
15	Jan 2006	Patrice Evra	£5.5m	
16	Jul 2007	Owen Hargreaves	£17.0m	
17	Jul 2007	Anderson	£20.4m	
18	Sep 2008	Dimitar Berbatov	£30.8m	
19	Jun 2009	Antonio Valencia	£16.0m	
20	Jul 2009	Michael Owen	free	

(Answers on page 142)

Name the Eleven...

... United players who started the 2008 Champions League final.

Match the players to the shirt number they wore that day

1 _____

6 _____

5 _____

15 _____

3 _____

4 _____

18 _____

16 _____

7 _____

10 _____

32 _____

(Answers on page 143)

Sir Bobby Charlton

1. In what year was was Sir Bobby Charlton born?
(a) 1934   (b) 1937   (c) 1940

2. Which famous footballer is Charlton related to?
(a) Stanley Matthews   (b) Tom Finney   (c) Jackie Milburn

3. How old was he when he joined United?
(a) 15   (b) 17   (c) 19

4. In which season did he make his United debut?
(a) 1954-55   (b) 1956-57   (c) 1958-59

5. In what year did he appear in his first FA Cup final?
(a) 1955   (b) 1957   (c) 1959

6. In what year did he win his only FA Cup?
(a) 1957   (b) 1960   (c) 1963

7. How many league titles did he win at United?
(a) two   (b) three   (c) four

8. How many times did he play for United?
(a) 558   (b) 658   (c) 758

9. How many goals did he score at United?
(a) 219   (b) 249   (c) 279

10. In what year did he win the Ballon d'Or?
(a) 1966   (b) 1968   (c) 1970

11. How many goals did he score in the 1966 World Cup finals?
(a) two   (b) three   (c) four

12. How many goals did he score in the 1968 European Cup Final?
(a) none   (b) one   (c) two

13. Which England player was arrested after going shopping with Charton during the 1970 World Cup finals?
(a) Geoff Hurst   (b) Jeff Astle   (c) Bobby Moore

14. Who was Charton substitued for in 1970 World Cup quarter-final v Germany?
(a) Martin Peters   (b) Colin Bell   (c) Alan Ball

15. How many England Caps did he earn?
(a) 96   (b) 106   (c) 116

16. How many times did he score for England?
(a) 37   (b) 43   (c) 49

17. At which club did he become player-manager after leaving United in 1973?
(a) Preston   (b) Stockport   (c) Wigan

18. Where did he finish his playing career?
(a) Tobermore United   (b) Carlisle United   (c) Waterford United

19. In what year did he join the Manchester United board?
(a) 1982   (b) 1984   (c) 1986

20. What honour did he receive in 1994?
(a) OBE   (b) CBE   (c) knighthood

(Answers on page 143)

Clean Sheets

Name the post-War United keepers who have kept the most clean sheets.

	Player	Country from	Years at Club	Total Apps	Clean Sheets
1		Denmark	1991-99	398	**180**
2		England	1966-78	539	**175**
3		England	1978-87	375	**161**
4		Spain	2011-	437	**155**
5		Holland	2005-11	266	**135**
6		England	1945-56	212	**67**
7		England	1949-59	208	**55**
8		France	2000-04	139	**50**
9		N. Ireland	1957-67	247	**44**
10		Argentina	2015-	61	**39**
11		N. Ireland	2001-05	72	**38**
12		Scotland	1988-91	94	**34**
13		USA	2003-07	77	**31**
14		Poland	2006-12	61	**28**
15		England	1950-53	80	**27**
16		Holland	1996-02	60	**27**
17		Eire	1964-66	67	**26**
18		England	1985-88	79	**24**
19		England	1986-95	63	**22**
20		England	1956-67	120	**21**

(Answers on page 144)

What's Eric done now?

Can you guess the offences that led to Eric Cantona incurring the wrath of the authorities?

1. Why did Auxerre fine him in 1987?
(a) he insulted the manager (b) he refused to be substituted (c) he punched a team-mate

2. What did he receive a three-month suspension for in 1988?
(a) a dangerous kung-fu tackle (b) head-butting an opponent (c) slapping a fan

3. Why was he banned from international matches for one year in 1988?
(a) he refused to sing the national anthem (b) he insulted national coach Henri Michel on TV (c) he punched a team-mate

4. Why did Marseilles ban him for a month following a friendly game against Torpedo Moscow in January 1989?
(a) he hit a fan (b) he tore up the referee's yellow card and called him a "bastard" (c) he kicked the ball at the crowd and threw his shirt away after being substituted

5. Why did six Montpellier players demand his sacking—resulting in him being banned from the training ground for ten days—when he was on loan there in the 1989-90 season?
(a) he threw his boots in a team-mate's face (b) he punched a team-mate (c) he smashed the windscreen of a team-mate's car

6. Why was he banned for one month by the French Football Federation in December 1991?
(a) he insulted the coach   (b) he threw the ball at a referee
(c) he refused to play in a friendly

7. Why was the ban doubled?
(a) he refused to answer their questions   (b) he told them he'd do it again   (c) because he walked up to each member of the hearing committee and called them an "idiot".

8. Why was he fined £1,000 by the FA in 1993?
(a) for slapping a Leeds fan   (b) for spitting at a Leeds fan
(c) for kicking the ball at a Leeds fan

9. Why was he banned for five matches in March 1994?
(a) for two successive red cards   (b) for violent conduct
(c) for insulting the FA

10. For what offence was he sentenced to 120 hours of community service in 1995?
(a) affray   (b) assault   (c) grevious bodily harm

(Answers on page 145)

Patrice Evra

1. In what year was Patrice Evra born?
(a) 1979   (b) 1981   (c) 1983

2. What was his father's profession?
(a) farmer   (b) engineer   (c) diplomat

3. What position did he play as a schoolboy?
(a) winger   (b) midfielder   (c) striker

4. In which league did he begin his playing career?
(a) Serie C   (b) Serie B   (c) Ligue 2

5. Which French club did United sign him from in 2006?
(a) Nice   (b) Monaco   (c) Marseilles

6. What was the fee?
(a) £5.5 million   (b) £8.5 million   (c) £11.5 million

7. With whom did he have an altercation following a game at Stamford Bridge in 2008 that resulted in a four-match ban?
(a) a steward   (b) a groundsman   (c) a journalist

8. What term did he use to describe Arsenal players following United's Champions League semi-final win over them in 2009?
(a) infants   (b) toddlers   (c) babies

9. How many games did he play for United?
(a) 279   (b) 379   (c) 479

10. How many United goals did he score?
(a) 10   (b) 15   (c) 20

11. How many Premier League titles did he win at United?
(a) three   (b) four   (c) five

12. What was the first trophy he won as United captain?
(a) 2009 League Cup   (b) 2010 League Cup   (c) 2011 Community Shield

13. Why did he receive a five-match international following the 2010 World Cup?
(a) for leading a player protest   (b) for insulting the coach   (c) for being friends with Eric Cantona

14. Which club did he join after leaving United in 2014?
(a) Inter Milan   (b) Juventus   (c) Porto

15. Where did he end his playing career?
(a) West Ham   (b) Marseilles   (c) Celtic

(Answers on page 145)

How Tall? (part 4)

Guess the heights of these former United players.

	Player	Years at club	Height
1	Ole Gunnar Solskjaer	1996–2007	
2	Teddy Sheringham	1997–2001	
3	Jaap Stam	1998–2001	
4	Dwight Yorke	1998–2002	
5	John O'Shea	1999–2011	
6	Fabien Barthez	2000–2004	
7	Ruud van Nistelrooy	2001–2006	
8	Rio Ferdinand	2002–2014	
9	Cristiano Ronaldo	2003–2009	
10	Wayne Rooney	2004–2017	
11	Park Ji-sung	2005–2012	
12	Patrice Evra	2006–2014	
13	Nani	2007–2015	
14	Dimitar Berbatov	2008–2012	
15	Antonio Valencia	2009–2019	
16	Chris Smalling	2010–2019	
17	Ashley Young	2011–2020	
18	Robin van Persie	2012–2015	
19	Marouane Fellaini	2013–2019	
20	Marcos Rojo	2014–2019	

Score half a point if you're an inch out either way. Half inches are rounded up.

(Answers on page146)

Anagrams: The Managers

Rearrange the letters to form the names of United managers (including caretakers).

1. Rank notions   ___ / _____

2. Analog visual   _____ / ___ / ____

3. Tabby tums   ____ / _____

4. Metric war clerk   _____ / _____

5. Texan doves   ____ / _____

6. Saggy ring   ____ / _____

7. Mangles lantern   _____ / _____

8. Korean solar jungles   ___ / _____ / _____

9. Cussing new film   ____ / _____

10. Moved daisy   _____ / _____

(Answers on page 146)

Transfers: The 2010s

Match the clubs to the United signings.

Ajax	Atletico Madrid	Crystal Palace	PSV Eindhoven
Anderlecht	Bayern Munich	Everton	Shaktar Donetsk
Arsenal	Benfica	Fulham	Southampton
Aston Villa	Blackburn	Leicester	Swansea
Athletic Bilbao	Chelsea	Monaco	Villarreal

	Date	Player	Fee	Signed from
1	Jan 2010	Chris Smalling	£12m	
2	Mar 2011	Adnan Januzaj	£0.6m	
3	Jun 2011	Phil Jones	£17.0m	
4	Jun 2011	Ashley Young	£16m	
5	Jun 2011	David De Gea	£18m	
6	Aug 2012	Robin van Persie	£24m	
7	Jan 2013	Wilfred Zaha	£10m	
8	Sep 2013	Marouane Fellaini	£27.5m	
9	Jan 2014	Juan Mata	£37.1m	
10	Jun 2014	Ander Herrera	£29m	
11	Jun 2014	Luke Shaw	£27m	
12	Aug 2014	Daley Blind	£13.8m	
13	Jun 2015	Memphis Depay	£31m	
14	Jul 2015	Bastian Schweinsteiger	£14.4m	
15	Aug 2015	Anthony Martial	£36m	
16	Jun 2016	Eric Bailly	£30m	
17	Jul 2017	Victor Lindelof	£31m	
18	Jun 2018	Fred	£47m	
19	Jun 2019	Daniel James	£15m	
20	Aug 2019	Harry Maguire	£80m	

(Answers on page 147)

Rio Ferninand

1. Where was Rio Ferdinand born?
(a) Brighton (b) London (c) Luton

2. At which sport did he represent his borough as a child?
(a) boxing (b) cricket (c) gymnastics

3. At which club did he make his Premier League debut?
(a) West Ham (b) Leeds (c) Crystal Palace

4. How old was he when he made his England debut?
(a) 18 years, 98 days (b) 19 years, 8 days (c) 19 years, 238 days

5. How much did Leeds pay for him in 2000?
(a) £14 million (b) £18 million (c) £22 million

6. When did he sign for United?
(a) July 2001 (b) July 2002 (c) January 2003

7. What was the fee?
(a) £25 million (b) £30 million (c) £35 million

8. What was unusual about his FA Cup quarter-final appearance against Portsmouth in March 2008?
(a) he took the corners (b) he played in midfield (c) he played in goal

9. What type of injury kept he out of the 2010 World Cup finals?
(a) knee (b) ankle (c) back

10. How many Premier League titles did he win at United?
(a) five (b) six (c) seven

11. How many games did he play for United?
(a) 455 (b) 505 (c) 555

12. How many United goals did he score?
(a) 4 (b) 8 (c) 12

13. How many England caps did he earn?
(a) 61 (b) 71 (c) 81

14. Which club did he join after leaving United in 2014?
(a) West Ham (b) Cardiff (c) QPR

15. Which professional sport did he announce he was taking up in September 2017?
(a) golf (b) boxing (c) squash

(Answers on page147)

George Best 2

1. How many games did George Best play for United?
(a) 370   (b) 470   (c) 570

2. In what season was he the First Division top scorer?
(a) 1965-66   (b) 1967-68   (c) 1969-70

3. How many Northern Ireland caps did he earn?
(a) 37   (b) 47   (c) 57

4. How many goals did he score for United?
(a) 139   (b) 159   (c) 179

5. Who did he spend the week with in 1971 instead of going to training?
(a) Miss Ireland   (b) Miss World   (c) Miss Great Britain

6. Why did he miss the train to Stamford Bridge in the 1971-72 season?
(a) to spent the weekend with an actress   (b) to open a boutique   (c) he overslept

7. What was the name of the Manchester nightclub he opened in 1973?
(a) Slim Jim   (b) Slack Alice   (c) Pips

8. In what year did he win the Ballon d'Or?
(a) 1968   (b) 1969   (c) 1970

9. Which was the first English club Best played for after leaving United?
(a) Oldham   (b) Stockport   (c) Bury

10. Which American club did he sign for in 1976?
(a) New York Cosmos   (b) San Jose Earthquakes   (c) Los Angeles Aztecs

11. At which club did he play alongside Rodney Marsh and Bobby Moore?
(a) Fulham   (b) QPR   (c) Brentford

12. Which Scottish club did he sign for in 1979?
(a) Hearts   (b) Aberdeen   (c) Hibernian

13. In what year was he given a three-month prison sentence?
(a) 1982   (b) 1984   (c) 1986

14. Where did he end his playing career?
(a) Tobermore United   (b) Brisbane Lions   (c) Bournemouth

15. How old was George Best when he died?
(a) 56   (b) 59   (c) 62

(Answers on page 148)

Shoot-outs 5

2018 League Cup third round
Old Trafford, Tue 25 Sep
United   2 -2   Derby

Lineup: Romero, Dalot, Bailly, Jones, Young, Herrera, Matic, Mata, Lingard, Martial, Lukaku,
Subs: Fred, Fellaini, Grant

Fill in in the names of United's penalty takers below

	United		7-8	Derby	
1		scored		Mount	scored
2		scored		Jozefzoon	scored
3		scored		Wilson	scored
4		scored		Marriot	scored
5		scored		Johnson	scored
6		scored		Bryson	scored
7		scored		Forsyth	scored
8		saved		Keogh	scored

Score half a point if you select a correct player but in the wrong order.

(Answers on page 149)

Ryan Giggs

1. Where was Ryan Giggs born?
(a) Manchester   (b) Swansea   (c) Cardiff

2. What professional sport did his father play?
(a) rugby union (b) rugby league   (c) hockey

3. At which club was he a youth team player before joining United, aged 14?
(a) Oldham   (b) Bolton   (c) Man City

4. In which season did he make his first-team debut?
(a) 1989-90   (b) 1990-91   (c) 1991-92

5. Who were the opponents when Giggs scored his first United goal?
(a) Man City   (b) Arsenal   (c) Liverpool

6. What was the name of TV show Giggs hosted that first aired in 1994?
(a) Giggs & Co   (b) Ryan Giggs' Soccer Skills   (c) Football Talk with Ryan Giggs

7. How many years did he spend in United's first team?.
(a) 19   (b) 21   (c) 23

8. How many appearances did he make for United?
(a) 763   (b) 863   (c) 963

9. How many goals did he score for United?
(a) 138   (b) 168   (c) 198

10. How many Wales caps did he earn?
(a) 64   (b) 84   (c) 104

11. How many Premier League titles did he win?
(a) 9   (b) 11   (c) 13

12. When was he named BBC Sports Personality of the Year?
(a) 2007   (b) 2009   (c) 2011

13. Who were the opponents for the goal that won Giggs the 1998-99 BBC Goal of the Season award?
(a) Arsenal   (b) Liverpool   (c) Aston Villa

14. In what year was he appointed United's assistant manager?
(a) 2013   (b) 2014   (c) 2015

15. What honour was he awarded in 2007?
(a) MBE   (b) OBE   (c) CBE

(Answers on page 149)

The Captains

Name the last ten players to be appointed United club captain.

	Year	Player
1	1994	
2	1996	
3	1997	
4	2005	
5	2011	
6	2014	
7	2017	
8	2018	
9	2019	
10	2019	

(Answers on page 149)

Answers

Answers: The Early Years

1. (b) Lancashire and Yorkshire
2. (a) 1878
3. (c) Frederick Attock
4. (a) North Road
5. (c) lost in the final (3–0 to Hurst at Whalley Range)
6. (c) four
7. (b) 1886-87
8. (b) 1892
9. (a) 1893
10. (b) 1902
11. (c) Manchester Central
12. (a) John Henry Davies
13. (b) brewer
14. (c) Ernest Mangnall
15. (c) 50,000
16. (a) Man City
17. (b) 1908
18. (b) 1910
19. (b) £60,000
20. (a) 1909

Answers: Name the Three

George Best, Denis Law and Sir Bobby Charlton

Answers: Eric Cantona

1. (b) 1966
2. (c) Spanish
3. (c) SO Caillolais
4. (a) goalkeeper
5. (c) so he could perform national service
6. (b) Auxerre
7. (c) his psychoanalyst
8. (a) 10 months
9. (b) £1.2
10. (c) 10
11. (a) Benfica (it was a friendly in Lisbon to mark Eusebio's 50th birthday)
12. (b) two (both pens)
13. (c) Galatasaray
14. (b) 9
15. (c) Richard Shaw
16. (b) 10 months
17. (a) 82
18. (b) 185
19. (c) French beach soccer team
20. (a) New York Cosmos

Answers: Where are they from?

1	David De Gea	Spain
2	Alex Telles	Brazil
3	Eric Bailly	Ivory Coast
4	Victor Lindelof	Sweden
5	Bruno Fernandes	Portugal
6	Fred	Brazil
7	Juan Mata	Spain
8	Nemanja Matic	Serbia

9	Paul Pogba	France
10	Donny van de Beek	Netherlands
11	Edinson Cavani	Uruguay
12	Anthony Martial	France

Answers: Transfers - The 1960s

	Player	Signed from
1	Noel Cantwell	West Ham
2	David Herd	Arsenal
3	Denis Law	Torino
4	Paddy Crerand	Celtic
5	Graham Moore	Chelsea
6	John Connelly	Burnley
7	Patrick Dunne	Everton
8	Alex Stepney	Chelsea
9	Willie Morgan	Burnley
10	Ian Ure	Arsenal

Answers: Name the Eleven…
… United players in the 1968 European Cup final

1	Alex Stepney
2	Shay Brennan
3	Tony Dunne
4	Pat Crerand
5	Bill Foulkes
6	Nobby Stiles
7	George Best
8	Brian Kidd
9	Bobby Charlton (capt)
10	David Sadler
11	John Aston

Answers: Sir Matt Busby

1. (b) 1909
2. (c) Man City (in 1934)
3. (b) Liverpool
4. (a) army
5. (a) one
6. (b) October 1945
7. (c) Blackpool
8. (c) Great Britain (in the 1948 Summer Olympics).
9. (b) 1951–52
10. (a) Real Madrid
11. (c) CBE
12. (c) Let It Be (in the track, "Dig It")
13. (a) 1969
14. (a) 1968
15. (c) president

Answers: Appearances

1	Ryan Giggs
2	Bobby Charlton
3	Paul Scholes
4	Bill Foulkes
5	Gary Neville
6	Wayne Rooney
7	Alex Stepney
8	Tony Dunne
9	Denis Irwin
10	Joe Spence

Answers: Who said that?

1. (c) Matt Busby
2. (a) Sir Alex Ferguson
3. (b) Ole Gunnar Solskjaer
4. (b) Eric Cantona
5. (a) Teddy Sheringham
6. (c) Sir Alex Ferguson
7. (b) Roy Keane
8. (c) David Gill
9. (a) Patrice Evra
10. (a) Sir Alex Ferguson
11. (b) Robin van Persie
12. (c) Rio Ferdinand
13. (b) Sir Alex Ferguson
14. (c) Matt Busby
15. (a) Patrice Evra

Answers: Name the 4

1	Alex Telles
2	Axel Tuanzebe
3	Anthony Martial
4	Luke Shaw

Answers: George Best

1. (b) Belfast
2. (c) for being too small and light
3. (b) 15
4. (a) Manchester Ship Canal
5. (b) 1963-64
6. (b) 5ft 9

7. (a) Burnley (on 28 Dec 1963. United won 5-1)
8. (c) 11
9. (a) Benfica
10. (b) the fifth Beatle ("O Quinto Beatle" in Portuguese. In English newspaers he was dubbed "El Beatle")
11. (c) FWA Footballer of the Year
12. by sleeping with a woman
13. (a) first
14. (b) six
15. (a) Northampton

Answers: How Tall?

	Player	Height
1	David de Gea	6ft 4
2	Victor Lindelof	6ft 2
3	Eric Bailly	6ft 2
4	Harry Maguire	6ft 4
5	Paul Pogba	6ft 3
6	Edinson Cavani	6ft 0
7	Juan Mata	5ft 7
8	Anthony Martial	5ft 11
9	Marcus Rashford	5ft 11
10	Mason Greenwood	5ft 11
11	Fred	5ft 7
12	Bruno Fernandes	5ft 10
13	Daniel James	5ft 7
14	Luke Shaw	6ft 1
15	Dean Henderson	6 ft 2
16	Alex Telles	5ft 11
17	Aaron Wan-Bissaka	6ft 0
18	Nemanja Matic	6ft 4
19	Donny van de Beek	6ft 0
20	Scott McTominay	6ft 4

Answers: Four or more

1	David Herd
2	Denis Law
3	George Best
4	Alan Gowling
5	Andrew Cole
6	Solskjaer, Ole-Gunnar
7	Ruud van Nistelrooy
8	Carlos Tevez
9	Wayne Rooney
10	Dimitar Berbatov

Answers: Shoot-outs

1	van Nistlerooy
2	Scholes
3	Rooney
4	Keane

Answers: Anagrams

1. Nobby Stiles
2. Denis Law
3. George Best
4. Alex Stepney
5. Gerry Daly
6. Stuart Pearson
7. Mickey Thomas
8. Ray Wilkins
9. Remi Moses
10. Gordon Strachan

Answers: Bryan Robson

1. (c) Durham
2. (a) West Brom
3. (b) 1981
4. (c) £1,500,000 (a Brirish record at the time)
5. (c) Arsenal
6. (b) two
7. (c) three
8. (a) (b) (c) seven years
9. (b) 461
10. (c) 99
11. (c) Middlesbrough
12. (b) Sheffield United
13. (a) Thailand
14. (b) Captain Marvel
15. (b) OBE

Answers: A Tricky One

1	Marcus Rashford
2	Anthony Martial
3	Zlatan Ibrahimovic
4	Robin van Persie
5	Shinji Kagawa
6	Dimitar Berbatov
7	Wayne Rooney
8	Michael Owen
9	Carlos Tevez
10	Cristiano Ronaldo
11	Ruud van Nistelrooy
12	Dwight Yorke
13	Teddy Sheringham

14	Paul Scholes
15	Andrew Cole
16	Andrei Kanchelskis
17	Mark Hughes
18	Lee Sharpe
19	Brian McClair
20	Jesper Olsen

Bonus question: Carlos Tevez

Answers: Name the Season

1. 1999-2000
2. 1982-83
3. 1970-71
4. 1991-92
5. 1984-85
6. 1976-77
7. 2002-03
8. 1980-81
9. 1992-93
10. 1988-89

Answers: 1999 Champions League

1. (c) LKS Lodz
2. (b) 3-3
3. (a) Scholes
4. (c) 11-2
5. (b) Keane
6. (a) Yorke
7. (b) 3-1
8. (b) 90+2

9. (c) 11mins
10. (b) 23mins
11. (c) Barcelona
12. (a) 90,245
13. (b) Stefan Effenberg
14. (b) 11mins
15. (c) Dwight Yorke (with 8 goals)

Answers: Goalscorers

	Name
1	Wayne Rooney
2	Bobby Charlton
3	Denis Law
4	Jack Rowley
5	Dennis Viollet
5	George Best
7	Joe Spence
7	Ryan Giggs
9	Mark Hughes
10	Paul Scholes

Answers: Wayne Rooney

1. (b) 1985
2. (c) 99
3. (b) 114
4. (b) 16 years 360 days
5. (b) 2002
6. (a) Aug 2004
7. (b) £25.6 million
8. (c) Fenerbahce

9. (a) 8
10. (c) sarcastic clapping
11. (c) 253
12. (b) 103
13. (c) 53
14. (a) 2009–10
15. (b) D.C United

Answers: Transfers - The 1970s

	Player	Signed from
1	Martin Buchan	Aberdeen
2	Ian Storey-Moore	Notts Forest
3	Wyn Davies	Man City
4	Ted MacDougall	Bournemouth
5	Alex Forsyth	Partick Thistle
6	George Graham	Arsenal
7	Jim Holton	Shrewsbury
8	Lou Macari	Celtic
9	Gerry Daly	Bohemians
10	Paddy Roche	Shelbourne
11	Stewart Houston	Brentford
12	Jim McCalliog	Wolves
13	Stuart Pearson	Hull
14	Gordon Hill	Millwall
15	Steve Coppell	Tranmere
16	Chris McGrath	Tottenham
17	Jimmy Greenhoff	Stoke
18	Joe Jordan	Leeds
19	Mickey Thomas	Wrexham
20	Ray Wilkins	Chelsea

Answers: Old Trafford

1. (c) John Henry Davies
2. (b) Archibald Leitch
3. (b) 80,000
4. (c) 19 February 1910
5. (a) Liverpool.
6. (a) 20,000
7. (b) 76,962 (set in March 1939)
8. (a) 1915 (the "Khaki Cup Final" between Sheffield United and Chelsea
9. (b) 1936
10. (c) 76,098 (for United v Blackburn in March 2007)
11. (a) 11,968 (v Fulham in April 1950)
12. (b) 2,197,429
13. (a) 1957
14. (a) 1965
15. (c) executive boxes
16. (c) 25,000
17. (b) £18.65m
18.) (c) Tottenham
19. (c) 2016
20. (a) 115 x 74 yards

Answers: Sir Alex Ferguson

1. (b) 1941
2. (c) Govan
3. (b) Chapman
4. (a) Queen's Park
5. (a) Fergie's
6. (c) East Stirlingshire
7. (b) 1976
8. (c) three (1979–80, 1983–84, 1984–85)
9. (b) November 1986

10. (c) Viv Anderson
11. (a) Wilfried Zaha
12. (c) for claiming the Champions League draw was fixed
13. (c) 13
14. (b) 1min 19secs
15. (c) 11
16. (c) 1,500
17. (a) Harvard
18. (c) the shipyard his father worked.
19. (b) 1999
20. (b) the JFK assassination (Fergie was sent 35 CDs on the subject by Gordon Brown and owns a copy of the Warren Report signed by Gerald Ford)

Answers: Name the Six

1. Brian and Jimmy Greenhoff
2. Martin and George Buchan
3. Gary and Phil Neville
4. Adam and Richard Eckersley
5. Rafael and Fabio Da Silva
6. Michael and Will Keane

Answers: Who wins at Scrabble?

Highest scores
1. Timothy Fosu-Mensah
2. Axel Tuanzebe
3. Donny van de Beek
4 & 5. (two from) Nemanja Matic, Marcus Rashford or Scott McTominay

Lowest scores
1. Fred

2. Diogo Dalot
3. Amad Diallo
4. Paul Pogba
5. Odion Ighalo

Answers: The Debut Goalscorers

1	Bobby Charlton
2	Denis Law
3	Lou Macari
4	Gordon Strachan
5	Neil Webb
6	Keith Gillespie
7	Paul Scholes
8	Ole-Gunnar Solskjaer
9	Ruud van Nistelrooy
10	Louis Saha
11	Wayne Rooney
12	Henrik Larsson
13	Federico Macheda
14	Javier Hernandez
15	James Wilson
16	Marcus Rashford
17	Zlatan Ibrahimovic
18	Romelu Lukaku
19	Daniel James
20	Donny van de Beek

Answers: Nobby Stiles

1. (c) Collyhurst
2. (a) an air raid
3. (b) 1960-61
4. (b) 395
5. (b) 19
6. (a) 28
7. (c) his false teeth
8. (a) none
9. (b) two
10. (a) 1971
11. (c) Middlesbrough
12. (c) Preston
13. (a) West Brom
14. (b) Johnny Giles
15. (a) MBE

Answers: How Tall? (part 2)

	Player	Height
1	Bobby Charlton	5ft 7
2	Nobby Stiles	5ft 6
3	Denis Law	5ft 9
4	George Best	5ft 9
5	Alex Stepney	6ft 0
6	Sammy McIlroy	5ft 10
7	Martin Buchan	5ft 10
8	Lou Macari	5ft 9
9	Gerry Daly	5ft 9
10	Brian Greenhoff	5ft 9
11	Arthur Albiston	5ft 7
12	Steve Coppell	5ft 6
13	Jimmy Greenhoff	5ft 10

14	Joe Jordan	6ft 1
15	Gordon McQueen	6ft 3
16	Mickey Thomas	5ft 6
17	Ray Wilkins	5ft 8
18	Remi Moses	5ft 6
19	Bryan Robson	5ft 10
20	Norman Whiteside	6ft 2

Answers: Shoot-outs 2

1	Tevez
2	Carrick
3	Ronaldo
4	Hargreaves
5	Nani
6	Anderson
7	Giggs

Answers: Anagrams 2

1. Charlie Mitten
2. Bill Foulkes
3. David Herd
4. Denis Law
5. Gerry Daly
6. Kevin Moran
7. Frank Stapleton
8. Norman Whiteside
9. Brian McClair
10. Lee Sharpe

Answers: Transfers - The 1980s

	Player	Signed from
1	Garry Birtles	Notts Forest
2	John Gidman	Everton
3	Frank Stapleton	Arsenal
4	Remi Mose	West Brom
5	Peter Beardsley	Vancover
6	Alan Brazil	Tottenham
7	Jesper Olsen	Ajax
8	Gordon Strachan	Aberdeen
9	Peter Barnes	Coventry
10	Colin Gibson	Aston Villa
11	Terry Gibson	Coventry
12	Viv Anderson	Arsenal
13	Brian McClair	Celtic
14	Steve Bruce	Norwich
15	Lee Sharpe	Torquay
16	Mark Hughes	Barcelona
17	Ralph Milne	Dundee United
18	Gary Pallister	Middlesbrough
19	Paul Ince	West Ham
20	Danny Wallace	Southampton

Answers: Name the Eleven...

... United players who started the 1991 Cup Winners' Cup final

1	Les Sealey
2	Denis Irwin
3	Clayton Blackmore
4	Steve Bruce
5	Mike Phelan

6	Gary Pallister
7	Bryan Robson (capt)
8	Paul Ince
9	Brian McClair
10	Mark Hughes
11	Lee Sharpe

Answers: The Glazers

1. (a) New York
2. (c) selling watches
3. (b) Tampa Bay Buccaneers
4. (b) £9 million
5. (a) Harry Dobson
6. (b) June 2005
7. (c) £660 million
8. (c) £62 million
9. (b) £265-£275 million
10. (b) 1931
11. (c) £716.5 million
12. (a) Red Knights
13. (b) 125,000
14. (c) £75 million ($110m)
15. (c) £129m ($200m)
16. (b) £56m ($73m)
17. (a) £42 million
18. (c) £948 million
19. (a) £70 million
20. (c) £455.5m (up 16% on the year)

Answers: Roy Keane

1. (b) Cork
2. (c) Cobh Ramblers

3. (a) £47,000
4. (b) 1993
5. (a) £3,750,000
6. (b) Crystal Palace
7. (a) 480
8. (b) 11
9. (b) 1997
10. (a) 51
11. (a) first
12. (c) 2000
13. (b) Celtic
14. (c) Sunderland
15. (a) Triggs

Answers: Record Signings

1	Martin Buchan
2	Ian Storey-Moore
3	Joe Jordan
4	Gordon McQueen
5	Ray Wilkins
6	Garry Birtles
7	Bryan Robson
8	Mark Hughes
9	Gary Pallister
10	Roy Keane
11	Andy Cole
12	Jaap Stam
13	Dwight Yorke
14	Ruud van Nistelrooy
15	Juan Sebastian Veron
16	Rio Ferdinand
17	Dimitar Berbatov
18	Juan Mata

19	Ángel Di María
20	Paul Pogba

Answers: Paul Scholes

1. (a) Salford
2. (c) 1993 (Scholes was too young to make the 1992 youth team)
3. (c) 24
4. (a) he scored both goals
5. (b) 1999-2000 (in the 7-1 win v West Ham in April)
6. (b) Bradford
7. (c) blurred vision
8. (b) deliberate handball
9. (c) New York Cosmos
10. (a) Man City
11. (b) 22 (the 18 shirt had been given to Ashley Young)
12. (c) 719
13. (b) 97
14. (c) 155
15. (b) 20
16. (c) 11 (1995–96, 1996–97, 1998–99, 1999–2000, 2000–01, 2002–03, 2006–07, 2007–08, 2008–09, 2010–11, 2012–13)
17. (a) 66
18. (a) Sweden
19. (b) April 2014 (following the sacking of Moyes)
20. (c) The Independent

Answers: Shoot-outs 3

1	Giggs
2	Tevez
3	Ronaldo

| 4 | Anderson |

Answers: 2008 Champions League

1. (b) Sporting CP
2. (a) Rooney
3. (c) 8-2
4. (c) 16
5. (a) Lyon
6. (b) 2-1
7. (c) with a header
8. (c) Tevez
9. (a) one
10. (b) Scholes
11. (c) Luzhniki Stadium
12. (a) Makelele
14. (a) Vidic
14. (b) Ronaldo
15. (c) Anelka

Answers: Denis Law

1. (a) Aberdeen
2. (b) Huddersfield
3. (b) £55,000 (then a British transfer record)
4. (c) Torino
5. (a) a car crash (teammate Joe Baker flipped the car over after driving the wrong way around a roundabout and was almost killed)
6. (c) £115,000
7. (b) 404
8. (c) 237
9. (a) his knee
10. (a) 1964

11. (c) 30
12. (c) Dennis Bergkamp (Dutch authorities refused to recognise the name unless it was spelt with two *n*'s as they felt it was too similar to *Denise*).
13. (a) one (in 1963)
14. (b) University of Aberdeen
15. (c) CBE

Answers: Hat-trick Kings

1	Denis Law
2	Jack Rowley
3	Dennis Viollet
4	Wayne Rooney
5	Bobby Charlton
6	Ruud van Nistelrooy
7	David Herd
8	Tommy Taylor
9	Andrew Cole
10	Alex Dawson
11	Dimitar Berbatov
12	Mark Hughes
13	George Best
14	Robin van Persie
15	Dwight Yorke
16	Ole-Gunnar Solskjaer
17	Andy Ritchie
18	Albert Quixall
19	Brian McClair
20	Paul Scholes

Answers: Anagrams 3

1. Gary Pallister
2. Gary Neville
3. Eric Cantona
4. Teddy Sheringham
5. Wes Brown
6. Jaap Stam
7. Mikael Silvestre
8. Ruud van Nistelrooy
9. Rio Ferdinand
10. Cristiano Ronaldo

Answers: Transfers - The 1990s

	Player	Signed from
1	Denis Irwin	Oldham
2	Andrei Kanchelskis	Shakhtar Donetsk
3	Peter Schmeichel	Brondby
4	Paul Parker	QPR
5	Dion Dublin	Cambridge United
6	Eric Cantona	Leeds
7	Roy Keane	Notts Forest
8	David May	Blackburn
9	Andy Cole	Newcastle
10	Ronny Johnsen	Besiktas
11	Ole Gunnar Solskjaer	Molde
12	Karel Poborsky	Slavia Prague
13	Jordi Cruyff	Barcelona
14	Teddy Sheringham	Tottenham
15	Henning Berg	Blackburn
16	Jonathan Greening	York City
17	Jaap Stam	PSV Eindhoven
18	Dwight Yorke	Aston Villa

19	Quentin Fortune	Atletico Madrid
20	Mickael Silvestre	Inter Milan

Answers: Name the XI...

... United players who started the 1999 Champions League final

1	Peter Schmeichel (capt)
2	Gary Neville
5	Ronny Johnsen
6	Jaap Stam
3	Denis Irwin
11	Ryan Giggs
7	David Beckham
8	Nicky Butt
15	Jesper Blomqvist
19	Dwight Yorke
9	Andy Cole

Answers: Gary Neville

1. (b) 1975
2. (a) cricket
3. (b) September 1992
4. (c) 2005
5. (b) 602
6. (b) Bolton
7. (a) 7
8. (c) 85
9. (b) 8
10. (b) 2012
11. (a) Northern Stock Exchange
12. (c) Salford City

13. (a) University of Salford
14. (b) Valencia
15. (b) *Red:* My *Autobiography*

Answers: Penalty Scorers

1	Ruud van Nistelrooy
2	Wayne Rooney
3	Bruno Fernandes
4	Albert Quixal
5	Eric Cantona
6	Steve Bruce
7	Charlie Mitten
8	Gerry Daly
9	Cristiano Ronaldo
10	Denis Law
11	Roger Byrne
12	Denis Irwin
13	George Best
14	Gordon Strachan
15	Bobby Charlton
16	Gordon Hill
17	Paul Pogba
18	Marcus Rashford
19	Willie Morgan
20	Brian McClair
21	Robin van Persie
22	Anthony Martial
23	Jack Picken
24	George Wall
25	Harry Rowley
26	Sammy McIlroy

27	Arnold Muhren
28	Jesper Olsen
29	Peter Davenport
30	Juan Mata

Answers: David Beckham

1. (b) Leytonstone
2. (c) United mascot
3. (b) 14th
4. (a) Crystal Palace
5. (c) Andrei Kanchelskis
6. (b) Preston
7. (a) scoring from a corner
8. (c) Leeds
9. (a) 0-0
10. (c) 10 (following Mark Hughes' departure)
11. (b) Neil Sullivan
12. (b) 13 (the highest in the League)
13. (a) 1998
14. (c) 437
15. (b) Deportivo de La Coruna
16. (c) 115
17. (b) six (1995–96, 1996–97, 1998–99, 1999–2000, 2000–01, 2002–03)
18. (b) 27
19. (c) PSG
20. (b) OBE

Answers: How Tall? (part 3)

	Player	Height
1	Jesper Olsen	5ft 6
2	Gordon Strachan	5ft 6
3	Brian McClair	5ft 10
4	Steve Bruce	6ft 0
5	Mal Donaghy	6ft 0
6	Gary Pallister	6ft 4
7	Paul Ince	5ft 10
8	Denis Irwin	5ft 8
9	Ryan Giggs	5ft 10
10	Andrei Kanchelskis	5ft 10
11	Paul Parker	5ft 7
12	Peter Schmeichel	6ft 3
13	Gary Neville	5ft 11
14	David Beckham	5ft 11
15	Nicky Butt	5ft 10
16	Eric Cantona	6ft 2
17	Roy Keane	5ft 10
18	Paul Scholes	5ft 6
19	Andy Cole	5ft 11
20	Phil Neville	5ft 11

Answers: Where are they from? (Part 2)

	Player	Country of Origin
1	Jesper Olsen	Denmark
2	Andrei Kanchelskis	Russia
3	Peter Schmeichel	Denmark
4	Eric Cantona	France
5	Ronny Johnsen	Norway
6	Ole Gunnar Solskjaer	Norway
7	Henning Berg	Norway

8	Jaap Stam	Netherlands
9	Dwight Yorke	Trinidad and Tobago
10	Quinton Fortune	South Africa
11	Mikael Silvestre	France
12	Fabien Barthez	France
13	Ruud van Nistelrooy	Netherlands
14	Cristiano Ronaldo	Portugal
15	Louis Saha	France
16	Edwin van der Sar	Netherlands
17	Park Ji-sung	South Korea
18	Patrice Evra	France
19	Nemanja Vidic	Serbia
20	Nani	Portugal
21	Anderson	Brazil
22	Dimitar Berbatov	Bulgaria
23	Rafael	Brazil
24	Antonio Valencia	Ecuador
25	Javier Hernandez	Mexico
26	Robin van Persie	Netherlands
27	Marouane Fellaini	Belgium
28	Daley Blind	Netherlands
29	Ander Herrera	Spain
30	Marcos Rojo	Argentina

Answers: Shoot-outs 4

1	Berbatov
2	Ferdinand
3	Vidic
4	Anderson

Answers: A Tricky One (part two)

1	Norman Whiteside
2	Frank Stapleton
3	Sammy McIlroy
4	Andy Ritchie
5	Lou Macari
6	Jimmy Greenhoff
7	Gordon Hill
8	Stuart Pearson
9	Gerry Daly
10	George Best
11	Alan Gowling
12	Willie Morgan
13	Denis Law
14	Bobby Charlton
15	David Herd
16	John Connelly
17	Albert Quixall
18	Norbert Lawton
19	Dennis Viollet
20	Alex Dawson

Answers: Name the Season 2

1. 1994-95
2. 1985-86
3. 2004-05
4. 1987-88
5. 1993-94
6. 1972-73
7. 2006-07

8. 1990-91
9. 1986-87
10. 1995-96

Answers: Six or more

1	Barnsley
2	Sheffield Wed
3	Brondby
4	Leicester
5	Notts Forest
6	West Ham
7	Bradford
8	Arsenal
9	Southampton
10	West Ham
11	Newcastle
12	Fenerbahce
13	Roma
14	Newcastle
15	Blackburn
16	Arsenal
17	Tranmere
18	Leeds
19	Southampton
20	Roma

Answers: Anagrams 4

1. Louis Saha
2. Edwin van der Sar
3. Patrice Evra
4. Anderson
5. Chris Smalling
6. Phil Jones
7. Robin van Persie
8. Daley Blind
9. Eric Bailly
10. Mason Greenwood

Answers: Transfers - The 2000s

	Player	Signed from
1	Fabien Barthez	Monaco
2	Ruud Van Nistelrooy	PSV Eindhoven
3	Juan Sebastian Veron	Lazio
4	Roy Carroll	Wigan
5	Diego Forlan	Atletico Independiente
6	Rio Ferdinand	Leeds
7	David Bellion	Sunderland
8	Eric Djemba-Djemba	Nantes
9	Cristiano Ronaldo	Sporting Lisbon
10	Louis Saha	Fulham
11	Gabriel Heinze	PSG
12	Ji-Sung Park	PSV Eindhoven
13	Ben Foster	Stoke
14	Nemanja Vidic	Spartak Moscow
15	Patrice Evra	Monaco
16	Owen Hargreaves	Bayern Munich
17	Anderson	Porto
18	Dimitar Berbatov	Tottenham

| 19 | Antonio Valencia | Wigan |
| 20 | Michael Owen | Newcastle |

Answers: Name the XI…

… United players who started the 2008? Champions League final

1	Edwin van der Sar
6	Wes Brown
5	Rio Ferdinand (capt)
15	Nemanja Vidic
3	Patrice Evra
4	Owen Hargreaves
18	Paul Scholes
16	Michael Carrick
7	Cristiano Ronaldo
10	Wayne Rooney
32	Carlos Tevez

Answers: Sir Bobby Charlton

1. (b) 1937
2. (c) Jackie Milburn
3. (a) 15
4. (b) 1956-57
5. (b) 1957
6. (c) 1963
7. (b) three (1956–57, 1964–65, 1966–67)
8. (c) 758
9. (b) 249
10. (a) 1966
11. (b) three

12. (c) two
13. (c) Bobby Moore
14. (b) Colin Bell
15. (b) 106
16. (c) 49
17. (a) Preston
18. (c) Waterford United
19. (b) 1984
20. (c) knighthood

Answers: Clean Sheets

1	Peter Schmeichel
2	Alex Stepney
3	Gary Bailey
4	David de Gea
5	Edwin van der Sar
6	Jack Crompton
7	Ray Wood
8	Fabien Barthez
9	Harry Gregg
10	Sergio Romero
11	Roy Carroll
12	Jim Leighton
13	Tim Howard
14	Tomasz Kuszczak
15	Reg Allen
16	Raimond van der Gouw
17	Patrick Dunne
18	Chris Turner
19	Gary Walsh
20	David Gaskell

Answers: What's Eric done now?

1. (c) he punched a team-mate
2. (a) a dangerous kung-fu tackle
3. (b) for insulting national coach Henri Michel on TV
4. (c) he kicked the ball at the crowd and threw his shirt away after being substituted
5. (a) he threw his boots in a team-mate's face
6. (b) he threw the ball at a referee (
7. (c) because he walked up to each member of the hearing committee and called them an "idiot".
8. (b) for spitting at a Leeds fan
9. (a) for two successive red cards (against Swindon Town and Arsenal).
10. (b) assault

Answers: Patrice Evra

1. (b) 1981
2. (c) diplomat
3. (c) striker
4. (a) Serie C
5. (b) Monaco
6. (a) £5.5 million
7. (b) a groundsman
8. (c) babies (the full quote was, "It was 11 men against 11 babies")
9. (b) 379
10. (a) 10
11. (c) five (2006–07, 2007–08, 2008–09, 2010–11, 2012–13)
12. (b) 2010 League Cup
13. (a) for leading a player protest
14. (b) Juventus
15. (a) West Ham

Answers: How Tall? (part 4)

	Player	Height
1	Ole Gunnar Solskjaer	5ft 10
2	Teddy Sheringham	6ft 1
3	Jaap Stam	6ft 3
4	Dwight Yorke	5ft 9
5	John O'Shea	6ft 3
6	Fabien Barthez	5ft 11
7	Ruud van Nistelrooy	6ft 2
8	Rio Ferdinand	6ft 2
9	Cristiano Ronaldo	6ft 2
10	Wayne Rooney	5ft 10
11	Park Ji-sung	5ft 9
12	Patrice Evra	5ft 8
13	Nani	5ft 10
14	Dimitar Berbatov	6ft 2
15	Antonio Valencia	5ft 11
16	Chris Smalling	6ft 4
17	Ashley Young	5ft 9
18	Robin van Persie	6ft 0
19	Marouane Fellaini	6ft 6
20	Marcos Rojo	6ft 2

Answers: Anagrams - The Managers

1. Ron Atkinson
2. Louis van Gaal
3. Matt Busby
4. Walter Crickmer
5. Dave Sexton
6. Ryan Giggs
7. Ernest Mangnall
8. Ole Gunnar Solskjaer

9. Wilf McGuinness
10. David Moyes

Answers: Transfers - The 2010s

	Player	Signed from
1	Chris Smalling	Fulham
2	Adnan Januzaj	Anderlecht
3	Phil Jones	Blackburn
4	Ashley Young	Aston Villa
5	David De Gea	Atletico Madrid
6	Robin van Persie	Arsenal
7	Wilfred Zaha	Crystal Palace
8	Marouane Fellaini	Everton
9	Juan Mata	Chelsea
10	Ander Herrera	Athletic Bilbao
11	Luke Shaw	Southampton
12	Daley Blind	Ajax
13	Memphis Depay	PSV Eindhoven
14	Bastian Schweinsteiger	Bayern Munich
15	Anthony Martial	Monaco
16	Eric Bailly	Villarreal
17	Victor Lindelof	Benfica
18	Fred	Shaktar Donetsk
19	Daniel James	Swansea
20	Harry Maguire	Leicester

Answers: Rio Ferdinand

1. (b) London
2. (c) gymnastics
3. (a) West Ham
4. (b) 19 years, 8 days

5. (b) £18 million
6. (b) July 2002
7. (b) £30 million (a British transfer record)
8. (c) he played in goal (after replacement keeper Tomasz Kuszczak had been sent off)
9. (a) knee
10. (b) six
11. (a) 455
12. (b) 8
13. (c) 81
14. (c) QPR
15. (b) boxing

Answers: George Best 2

1. (b) 470
2. 1967-68
3. (a) 37
4. (c) 179
5. (c) Miss Great Britain
6. (a) to spent the weekend with an actress (Sinead Cusack, who later married Jeremy Irons)
7. (b) Slack Alice
8. (a) 1968
9. (b) Stockport
10. (c) Los Angeles Aztecs
11. (a) Fulham
12. (c) Hibernian
13. (b) 1984
14. (a) Tobermore United
15. (b) 59

Answers: Shoot-outs 5

1	Lukaku
2	Young
3	Fellaini
4	Fred
5	Martial
6	Dalot
7	Matic
8	Phil Jones

Answers: Ryan Giggs

1. (c) Cardiff
2. (a) rugby union
3. (c) Man City
4. (b) 1990-91
5. (a) Man City
6. (b) Ryan Giggs' Soccer Skills
7. (c) 23
8. (c) 963 (a club record)
9. (b) 168
10. (a) 64
11. (c) 13
12. (b) 2009
13. (a) Arsenal
14. (b) 2014
15. (b) OBE

Answers: The Captains

1	Steve Bruce
2	Eric Cantona
3	Roy Keane

4	Gary Neville
5	Nemanja Vidic
6	Wayne Rooney
7	Michael Carrick
8	Antonio Valencia
9	Ashley Young
10	Harry Maguire

How did you do?

	Max Score	Your Score
The Early Years	20	
Name the Three	3	
Eric Cantona	20	
Where are they from?	12	
Transfers - The 1960s	10	
Name the XI	11	
Sir Matt Busby	15	
Appearances	10	
Who said that?	15	
Name the Four	4	
George Best	15	
How Tall?	20	
Four or more	10	
Shoot-outs	4	
Anagrams	10	
Bryan Robson	15	
A Tricky One	20 (+5)	
Name the Season	10	
1999 Champions League	15	
Goalscorers	10	
Wayne Rooney	15	
Transfers - The 1970s	20	
Old Trafford	20	
Sir Alex Ferguson	20	
Name the Six	6	
Who Wins at Scrabble?	10	
The Debut Goalscorers	20	
Nobby Stiles	15	
How Tall? (part 2)	20	
Shoot-outs 2	7	
Anagrams 2	10	
Transfers - The 1980s	20	

Name the XI: 1991 CWC final	11
The Glazers	20
Roy Keane	15
Record Signings	20
Paul Scholes	20
Shoot-outs 3	4
2008 Champions League	15
Denis Law	15
Hat-trick Kings	20
Anagrams 3	10
Transfers - The 1990s	20
Name the XI: 1999 CL	11
Gary Neville	15
Penalty Scorers	30
David Beckham	20
How Tall? (part 3)	20
Where are they from? (Part 2)	30
Shoot-outs 4	4
A Tricky One (part two)	20
Name the Season 2	10
Six or more	20
Anagrams 4	10
Transfers - The 2000s	20
Name the XI: 2008 CL final	11
Sir Bobby Charlton	20
Clean Sheets	20
What's Eric done now?	10
Patrice Evra	15
How Tall? (part 4)	20
Anagrams: The Managers	10
Transfers - The 2010s	20
Rio Ferdinand	15
George Best 2	15
Shoot-outs 5	8
Ryan Giggs	15
The Captains	10
Total	**1,000**

Final Score

850 to 1,000
You're a United Legend—the pride of Old Trafford.

700 to 849
Impressive. You're the stuff that Premier League winners are made of.

550 to 699
Congratulations—you're a First Team regular.

400 to 549
Your hard work has not gone unnoticed. You've earned a League debut.

250 to 399
Showing promise. You're on the bench for the League Cup games.

under 250
Report for double training.

If you enjoyed this book it would be great if you could give it a rating, or leave a review, on Amazon.

Ratings and reviews make the book more visible, which helps improve sales.

Thanks,

Danny.